New London Interiors

Kieran Long

New London Interiors

MERRELL

LONDON · NEW YORK

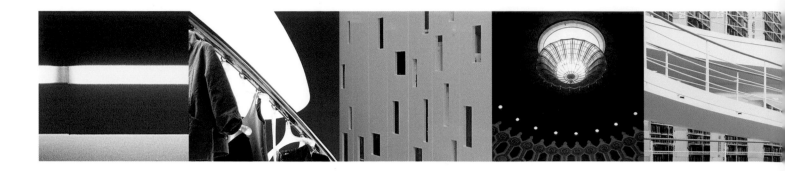

Introduction

BELOW London minimalism at its height: one of John Pawson's stores for Jigsaw.
OPPOSITE Joseph on Sloane Street, designed by David Chipperfield, with its
signature staircase.

London is a city that, within relatively recent memory, has woken up to contemporary design in a big way. The city's aesthetic traditionally had a nice line in kitsch – Formica café interiors, brass-bedecked pubs, the down-at-heel pie-and-mash shops and chop houses – but had never really set the agenda in terms of contemporary interior design. London lagged behind Paris, Milan and New York as a place where avant-garde interiors were commissioned and designed. Despite being a major world metropolis, there had always been something conservative about interior design in twentieth-century London, and a suspicion of playful and performative interior design, particularly in public and government buildings.

In the 1990s, the city saw a positive shift in its profile as a cultural and style capital. British artists such as Damien Hirst and Rachel Whiteread became global celebrities, London Fashion Week briefly rivalled Paris and New York and British designers such as Alexander McQueen, Stella McCartney and Hussein Chalayan were praised around the world but remained in the city. As *Vanity Fair* magazine famously proclaimed in March 1997, London was swinging again.

Around the same time, London design started to find its own ego, and the talent that had always been produced by the city's schools of architecture and design began to find work here to match their international profiles. It was in the early 1990s that 'London minimalism' emerged, a term that referred to the work of such architects as John Pawson, David Chipperfield, Claudio Silvestrin and Seth Stein, whose style defined cool, minimal interiors in many different contexts. The look consists of large and meticulous expanses of white surfaces, with moments of material quality, creating cool yet luxurious interiors that focus attention on products as if they were artworks in a gallery. This aesthetic became, in a sense, London's own, and minimalism entered the popular lexicon as a catch-all label for contemporary interior design. Pawson and Chipperfield had the right mix of artistic clients and commercial nous to turn a style into something much more influential and give London a much-needed identity. For both of them, their early big breaks came in the form of commissions from major fashion designers: Chipperfield designed a chain of stores around the world for Dolce & Gabbana, and Pawson produced his seminal Calvin Klein stores in Tokyo and New York. This led on to high-profile work on interiors in London, including a Chipperfield-designed store for fashion house Joseph on Sloane Street (1994) and Pawson's 1996 Jigsaw stores.

London's sheer size and its developing position as a crossroads for different cultural and commercial disciplines meant that further commissions came from a symbiosis between the worlds

of architecture and visual art. Pawson's 1988 studio for Michael Craig-Martin is a good example of this, as is Chipperfield's 1990 house for Antony Gormley and his later house for photographer Nick Knight. There has always been a close relationship between the worlds of architecture, fashion and art, and nowhere more so than in 1990s London.

London's smaller commercial galleries have a very healthy record of commissioning good interiors and buildings. Private galleries diversified in the 1990s, moving away from their traditional West End home and spreading across the capital, most notably to the east of London in an area that stretches from the Whitechapel Gallery on Whitechapel Road to the White Cube gallery on Hoxton Square. (In early 2004, the Whitechapel Gallery itself commissioned Belgian architects Robbrecht & Daem to work on the extension and refurbishment of their existing galleries.)

Charles Saatchi's gallery in St John's Wood, with the famous pool-of-oil installation by Richard Wilson.

Broadly speaking, there have been two trends in the design of private galleries. The first stems directly from Tony Fretton's small but highly influential building for the Lisson Gallery in Bell Street, Marylebone (1992). Each of the four floors of the Lisson is a single room, glazed to the north to provide consistent indirect light. The informal proportions and spare detailing give the top two floors an idiosyncratic but substantial presence on the street. The bottom two floors are fully glazed, situating the art in the city and allowing views in, particularly at night. The gallery is emphatically urban – it is no hermetic white box. In this lineage are Caruso St John's gallery for New York art dealer Larry Gagosian near King's Cross station, and Eric Parry's Timothy Taylor Gallery in the West End (see pages 136–37). Fretton's own project for Camden Arts Centre (see pages 120–21) reveals how far his work has come since completing the Lisson in 1992, but still demonstrates how much can be done with a limited budget to open up art institutions to the outside world.

The other strong strand of interior design for contemporary art space in London is the found space. This was inspired in the first instance by the New York loft scene of the 1970s, in which industrial spaces were taken over by artists for use as studios and galleries. Art mogul Charles Saatchi's gallery in St John's Wood was one of the first high-profile examples in London, and he combined it with an immense professionalism in the way in which exhibitions were presented, raising standards for art galleries in this country. The building, an old warehouse on Boundary Road, was converted in 1985 by architect Max Gordon, who retained the unadorned trusswork for public view, but skinned the uneven brickwork of the walls with smooth, white surfaces that concealed services and created storage space in the cavity behind them. The floor was painted gun-metal grey and the huge space was left completely uninterrupted by furniture. It was very much a cleaned-up loft-like space. The first show there was, appropriately enough, an exhibition of Minimal and Pop art from New York, further emphasizing the relationship between Saatchi and the gallery scene of New York in the 1970s and 1980s. American writer Kenneth Baker described entering the Saatchi Gallery as stepping "out of England in some denationalised zone of the intercontinental Art World, where the art-in-itself is fully manifest and all else is mere abstraction".

Many more former warehouses or industrial buildings have since been appropriated to make exhibition space, and the look is now familiar – a kind of generic, art-world cool that resides in the grand volumes and down-at-heel materials of these industrial buildings. Such galleries as the Victoria Miro, the Wapping Project (see pages 140–41) and White Cube in Shoreditch all continue the themes of the original Saatchi Gallery, and one could even say that it prepared the ground for the biggest found space of them all – Tate Modern. As David Chipperfield says, "The Saatchi Gallery was one of the first to say that you just need raw space, natural light and some artificial lighting." Ever ahead of the curve, Saatchi has now closed his St John's Wood location and opened a new gallery in the old County Hall on the South Bank (see pages 132–33), a move that has divided critical opinion but given new life to the Edwardian interiors of this neglected building – perhaps signalling a shift away from minimalism as the dominant aesthetic.

Whether Saatchi's St John's Wood gallery was as neutral as Chipperfield asserts is debatable. For all the apparent simplicity of the space, the gallery was very self-conscious in its references to its New York forebears. Found-space galleries are now common, and the influence of Saatchi and Tate Modern can be seen in other British cities, such as Newcastle's Baltic gallery situated in an old warehouse and in Cardiff, where architect Caruso St John has come up with a similar project called the Cardiff Depot, a new arts venue planned as the Welsh capital's Visual Arts Forum. These newer locations are attempting to reclaim the original philosophy of the found space, which had its earliest examples in London. Matt's

Gallery in Mile End (which opened in 1979) is often quoted as one of the earliest examples in the city, and remains a location in which artists can both develop their work and display it.

However, architect-designed spaces for artists are not always so successful and popular. When Anglo-French architect Decoi won the job of making an interior for the Blue Gallery in Clerkenwell, most thought it would be the first chance for the practice to realize a built manifestation of its radical tectonics in London. The interior had been planned as an undulating landscape of moulded plaster on walls and columns, but in 2000, with the gallery nearing completion, the client demolished the work while the architect was out of the country. The client and artists decided that the architecture was beginning to take precedence over the art, so they destroyed the interior, replacing it with a more conventional white-walled finish.

Most young architects' dream commission is for a new-build contemporary art gallery. There are few opportunities for this, and many have to make do with creating temporary installations for exhibitions. The large public galleries increasingly employ interesting younger architects to do this, and these installations have become an important medium in their own right. Good recent examples include Jamie Fobert's black steel trays and screens for Tate Modern's *The Upright Figure* exhibition in 2002, and Caruso St John's dense curation of *The Phantom Museum* exhibition at the British Museum in 2003. However, it is still in the private galleries that the most interesting exhibition design seems to be happening.

London-based architect David Adjaye, one of the hottest young architects in Europe, is probably the most in demand for exhibition design. His collaboration with artist Chris Ofili at the Victoria Miro Gallery in 2002 was a spectacular success, adding to his burgeoning profile and reputation. Ofili and Adjaye constructed a large room in the upper gallery to show thirteen of Ofili's works. The entrance was through a walnut-veneered corridor, a space of anticipation before the gallery itself, which was semi-lit at floor level, giving it a mystical, chapel-like atmosphere. Each painting was individually lit and supported on pieces of animal dung – one of the painter's trademarks. Three walnut-veneer benches sat in the room, and Adjaye cleverly played tricks with the viewer's sense of perspective, rounding off far corners of the room to make it seem bigger than it was. Adjaye is one of the premier stylists in British architecture, but with this project he showed that there is method to his sense of theatre, making a contemplative and unsettling room in which to display Ofili's paintings.

London interiors are not all sensitive minimalism, however. Although this may be the dominant idiom in art galleries and

some fashion stores, the diversity in retail and restaurant architecture is one of the most visible signs that contemporary interior design is fully accepted by the mainstream. Perhaps the most significant herald of this was the new McDonald's restaurant that opened on Upper Regent Street in late 2003, not fifty paces from where the statue of John Nash, the man who planned Regent Street in the 1810s, stands. While most of the projects you will see in these pages are bespoke interiors commissioned by clients who already value design, the new contemporary-style McDonald's shows that the accumulation of these projects is beginning to affect the commercial mainstream.

The new restaurant stands behind minimally detailed planar glass, and inside are all the trappings of a certain kind of generic contemporary interior design. Ikea-influenced plywood shelves and bars play a part in this aesthetic, as does a diversity of seating areas – low loungers in which to read your paper while sipping a coffee; bar seating by the windows for those in a hurry; and more conventional tables for the traditionalists among us. There are bold colours, contemporary fonts for lettering, and irregular areas of different flooring materials, denoting various zones of occupation in the interior. It owes more to the Starbucks model of corporate environments that attempt to reflect their customers' personalities than to the familiar fast-food restaurant interior of easy-to-clean beige Formica and fixed seating.

A new type of urban experience is demanded by the twenty-first-century consumer. The citizens of and visitors to a major Western metropolis are comfortable with the notion of cultural difference. The days when McDonald's served as an unofficial US embassy are gone – we no longer need respite from the culture of the city outside the doors. So, corporations are offering their consumers an idealized version of the experiences available in the city. We want to feel as if we are getting an authentic urban experience, and the multinationals are happy to give us what we want.

The rash of new coffee bars is probably the most visible of retail trends of the last few years in London, and they have begun to rival pubs as our favourite places in which to meet and relax in the city. The most ubiquitous of these, Starbucks, is an abstraction of a Seattle coffee bar – an ersatz creation that attempts to package a piece of urban sophistication for the consumer. Starbucks now has over 7200 stores worldwide, all serving the same product but attempting to provide a universal version of the comfort and intimacy of the American coffee shop. The emphasis here is on the consumer's individual experience rather than on the product alone. When we walk into a Starbucks we are invited to think about our lifestyle in a certain fashion – as connoisseurs of good coffee, as sophisticated people who need a caffeine fix from a convenient and reliable source.

Why is this? Images in the media increasingly value a certain type of experience as the quintessential life of the city dweller. This can be seen in such TV programmes as the American sitcom *Friends*, and depends on an increased acceptance of communal living, with groups of friends replacing the family as the primary social unit. The single person is acceptable in society, and has a high disposable income and large amounts of leisure time. This leads inexorably to the appropriation of commercial outlets as an extension of the domestic environment. Coffee shops typify this, allowing for a certain level of intimacy and a degree of self-expression in a communal environment. It exemplifies a certain middle-class urban experience – you can see the street, but the poor can't bother you if they can't afford the price of a cappuccino.

Other corporations have begun to convince us that every internal environment – commercial, cultural, corporate, hotel or residential – should project the values with which we, as consumers, would like to be associated, and provide a multi-faceted 'experience' rather than a simple retail outlet. Niketown on Oxford

The customer experience offered by Niketown is the biggest example yet of a new approach to retail.

Circus, designed by architect Building Design Partnership and completed in 2000, was the first, and it remains the most expansive example. Although Niketown is a shop, a huge proportion of its ample floor area – at some of the most expensive commercial rents in the West End – is given over to space for events, performances and permanent exhibits about the history of the corporation. With its huge, full-height atrium and stage-lit interior, it is, indeed, a shrine at which consumers can commune with one of the most successful of contemporary brands.

It is still in smarter high street stores that most innovation in interior design can be found. This is not on the level of creating new interiors that contribute as civic spaces, but as places that take the values of a brand and turn them into sublime pieces of theatre. Retail design is currently seeing a resurgence of the kinds of patronage that saw the creation of such retail temples as Galeries Lafayette in Paris, Selfridges on Oxford Street, London, KaDeWe in Berlin and Bullock's Wilshire in New York.

The contemporary version of this trend does not involve department stores, however, but individual brands and labels. The first to move in this direction was the Fiorucci store in New York in the 1970s and 1980s. Fiorucci became more than just a shop. It turned itself into the centre of a lifestyle, and a clubhouse for the young and fashionable. Fiorucci was founded in 1976 on East 59th Street and became a magnet for designers, models, trendspotters, buyers and stylists. Fashion designer Marc Jacobs says: "When I was fifteen, instead of going to sleep-away camp I spent the whole summer hanging out in the store." London's equivalent was probably Sex, a shop run by Malcolm McLaren and fashion designer Vivienne Westwood in the 1970s. The shop, at 430 King's Road, Chelsea, was the hub of the punk scene, and is now synonymous more with a way of life than with a product.

Both of these examples had a brand of cool that no amount of marketing and advertising could buy, and attempts are now being made to create this kind of brand equity again. Globally, the most important patron of this trend is Miuccia Prada, style icon and head of the Prada fashion house. She commissioned two of the world's most famous architects to create new flagship stores for Prada. Dutch architect Rem Koolhaas took on the New York commission, and Herzog & de Meuron, the architects of Tate Modern, created a crystalline new building in Tokyo. Koolhaas's project is an incredibly expensive fit-out of a former industrial building, which attempts to fuse a boutique with a performance and social space. A large excavated area lined in timber can be unfolded to reveal a stage, mixing fashion with culture and blurring the boundaries of what we expect from a store in the twenty-first century.

Rem Koolhaas's Prada store in New York is the first of Prada's Epicenter stores and points the way forward for prestige brands.

Prada New York incorporates a display system that doubles as a theatre for events.

RIGHT The Great Court of the British Museum, Europe's largest covered public space.

Office buildings in the major commercial cities of the world, and many of those featured here, exhibit a similar tendency, making the working environment accommodate a lifestyle rather than just providing a desk and a computer. The dotcom boom of the 1990s magnified existing trends in working practices. Staff turnovers are higher than they have ever been, and employees now look for more than just a salary when shopping for jobs. Also, office interiors are as much a part of the coherent branding of a corporation as its letterhead. So we see offices attempting to express a company's brand to clients – Harper Mackay's design for Valtech's offices in Clerkenwell (see pages 230–31) is a good example – and accommodating the lifestyles of creative employees, such as Urban Salon's exuberant interior for advertising agency Bartle Bogle Hegarty, with its eclectic materials and relaxed breakout areas and lounges.

This eliding of corporate and public space is one of the defining phenomena of contemporary cities. The trend stretches from Nike sponsoring basketball courts on east London council estates to the selling of franchises for cafés and shops in our major museums. In London, however, we are only just beginning to feel comfortable with using this type of combined space. The commercial interior spaces of Paris or Milan have a generosity about them that could be called public, despite, or perhaps because of, their devotion to commerce. Milan's Galleria Vittorio Emanuele II, a spectacular glass-roofed arcade, was constructed almost a century and a half ago and still provides sumptuous retail space while making physical and symbolic connections in the city. The galleria connects the cathedral square and the square in front of La Scala opera house with a commercial artery, creating the basis of an urban grain that is the envy of any city in the world.

The German philosopher and writer Walter Benjamin called the arcades of Paris "the most important architecture of the nineteenth century", and added that this architecture formed the gateway to the "primal landscape of consumption". His analysis of arcades focuses on their use of internal surfaces

(glass and marble) and the technology of display (kaleidoscopes, stereopticons) to manipulate consumers. There are cities in the UK that have networks of arcades. Leeds has its ornate Grand Arcade and County Arcade, and Cardiff has its less ornate, warren-like High Street and Duke Street arcades, among others. In these cities, such commercial interiors have set an enduring precedent for development, encouraging a mix of mall-like spaces that create a dense network of pedestrian links. The significant colonnades of London are usually small-scale, such Mayfair's Royal Arcade, but the arcade is being slowly rediscovered as developers look for ways of making the most of backlands areas of buildings. New arcades, shopping courtyards and covered markets are being rediscovered or built anew from Carnaby Street to Southwark.

Other new major public spaces in London are the many arts institutions that have rethought themselves as places in which to meet, eat and drink, as well as places where one can consume culture. In 1988, the Victoria and Albert Museum's advertising campaign billed it as "an ace caff with a quite nice museum attached". At the time, there was outcry about the cheapening of one of the greatest museums of the world; however, it signalled a significant change in the way we see our cultural institutions. This phenomenon – dubbed "café creep" by Harvard professor of urban design Jerold Kayden – profoundly affected the architecture of many of the cultural buildings completed in the boom years of the National Lottery, as institutions tried to find ways to give themselves some financial independence. All major cultural institutions in London now have prominent coffee shops and restaurants, radically changing how we see their interiors, arguably democratizing these traditionally elitist institutions and undeniably increasing the diversity of visitors.

The National Lottery has paid for some of the most significant contemporary interiors in London, including Foster and Partners' Great Court at the British Museum and the Turbine Hall of Tate Modern, designed by Herzog & de Meuron. The Great Court has been called London's greatest new public space, but unlike the city's other famous public spaces – the Royal Parks, Trafalgar

and let thy feet
millenniums hence
be set in midst of knowledge

OPPOSITE Norman Foster's steel-and-glass roof for the British Museum's Great Court creates the illusion of an exterior square without the inconvenience of the weather.
ABOVE LEFT The Turbine Hall of Tate Modern, by Herzog & de Meuron: another of London's recently acquired large-scale internal public spaces.
BELOW Sir Charles Barry's Reform Club (1841), one of the original bourgeois interior social spaces in London, based on an Italian palazzo but with a crystal roof above the courtyard.

Square, Leicester Square – it is covered with a glass roof. It has become London's best-known lottery-funded project, and Foster's renovation has transformed the experience of visitors, clearing the courtyard around the drum-shaped Reading Room and turning it into the museum's central orientation space.

The steel and glass of high-tech has been the dominant idiom in UK mainstream architecture for some years now, and the aesthetic can be seen in many of the works of such architects as Nicholas Grimshaw, Norman Foster, Richard Rogers and Michael Hopkins. The Great Court uses this approach to create a rare and welcome rain-free public space for tourists, touching the existing fabric of the building lightly. There are precedents for this kind of strategy, such as Rick Mather's glass roof on the sculpture garden of the Wallace Collection in Manchester Square, completed in 2000. However, the Great Court is on a much larger scale, and while it references classic London interiors, particularly Charles Barrie's Reform Club on Pall Mall, the courtyard's proportions and materials are those of a large-scale civic space such as an urban square. The Great Court, like Norman Foster's other masterwork, the Reichstag in Berlin, uses internal atriums and glazed spaces as if they were exteriors, attempting to elide the difference between inside and outside through the use of large areas of glass and light steel.

The other major internal public space completed in the last few years in London is in stark contrast to the Great Court: the Turbine Hall at Tate Modern, on the south bank of the Thames. Tate Modern occupies Sir Giles Gilbert Scott's Bankside power station, and was completed in 1999 by Herzog & de Meuron. Their design creates a warren of surprisingly small galleries behind the north façade of the building and provides a huge new public space in shape of the Turbine Hall, accessed from the north entrance or from the dramatic descending ramp in the west of the building. Tate Modern has been criticized for the quality of its gallery spaces, but the Turbine Hall is almost universally lauded. This huge volume – a floor area of 3,300 sq m (35,500 sq ft) – contains only the ticket office and a small mezzanine from which to enjoy frequently

OPPOSITE AND RIGHT The Wellcome Wing of the Science Museum by MacCormac Jamieson Prichard, funded by the National Lottery.

changing artistic installations. The Hall is undefined in terms of its use, but the installations it has already housed have challenged our conceptions of what it means to have a public interior on this scale. From Louise Bourgeois's steel towers, installed for the opening of the gallery, to Anish Kapoor's extraordinary fallopian-tube-like *Marsyas*, it has challenged artists to make public artworks on a scale rarely seen in this country. Witnessing people lying on the floor enjoying Olafur Eliasson's *Weather Project* in 2003 was to see a public space being used in an informal, relaxed and not terribly English way.

Many of the major cultural institutions in London have been given a revamp in the last few years, mostly thanks to money from the National Lottery: the glowing blue interior of the Wellcome Wing of the Science Museum by MacCormac Jamieson Prichard; the Royal Albert Hall's refurbishment, masterminded by architect BDP and including a new café/restaurant by Softroom (see pages 48–49); Tate Britain's Centenary Galleries by John Miller & Partners (see pages 134–35); the extension of the National Portrait Gallery and the refit of the Royal Opera House by Dixon Jones; and the Royal Festival Hall's refurbishment by Allies & Morrison, who also carried out the refit and extension of the Horniman Museum in south London. Most of these projects are successful reinterpretations of some of Britain's most significant buildings anywhere, and visitor numbers have increased immensely. One or two do not live up to expectations: Stanton Williams's controversial refit of the public areas of Denys Lasdun's National Theatre in the South Bank complex, for example, and HOK's extension to the Natural History Museum. Although few institutions have attempted to commission really radical architecture from outside the UK, two have shown the way

forward – Tate Modern and the Victoria and Albert Museum. The latter, which also commissioned Caruso St John's refurbishment of the Museum of Childhood (see pages 128–29), is still fighting for funding for its spiral extension designed by Daniel Libeskind.

Despite the profusion of design talent in London, the recent history of British domestic interiors is bound up with the profoundly British desire to customize surroundings ourselves, rather than trusting an interior designer or architect. Although there are designers of distinction in influential positions – Tom Dixon and Matthew Hilton at furniture store Habitat being two of the best placed to affect more mainstream tastes – there are few architects and interior designers who have the kind of profile that can affect the public at large. The interior designers with most influence are now those on television. The impact of Laurence Lewellyn-Bowen and an army of imitators cannot be under-estimated. With the rise of *Home Front* and other programmes like it, we are all now interior designers. With the help of a few bits of mdf and some lurid paint, we can all, according to *Home Front*'s website, create our own "Mexican style pink kitchen/diner" or "Asian décor neo-eclectic lounge".

The influence of television and the inexpensive contemporary furniture of Ikea has prompted a fundamental change in British domestic interiors. Even MFI, which remains the country's biggest furniture retailer, has had to think about modernizing due to stalling financial performance, and this can be traced directly back to a rising consciousness of contemporary design. Terence Conran, founder of Habitat and the Conran Design Partnership, has been brought in to rework MFI stores themselves, showing that his brand of contemporary design, once so boutique, has now reached a much wider audience.

William Morris's Arts and Crafts wallpaper designs were inspired by his very English brand of Socialism.

There is a tendency, because of television programmes and cheap furniture, to think that material quality and artistry have been replaced by mdf shapes and impermanent 'makeovers'. However, part of our fascination with these programmes does speak of a real history of interior design in this country that has always been as attracted to patterns, materials, fixtures and furnishings as it has to space-making.

The Arts and Crafts wallpaper patterns of William Morris are perhaps the quintessential example of this, and have become emblematic of the British interior. Morris's patterns, though, were at the time the very antithesis of the mass-produced coverings that dominate domestic interiors today. His patterns were hand-printed and beautifully intricate. Many, such as his Wey wallpaper, designed in 1884, are still in production today. However, Morris was also a Communist, and his decoration was part of a philosophy that saw decorative arts as a part of a broader Socialist struggle. In his lecture 'Art and Socialism', delivered to the Leicester Secular Society in 1884, he expanded his theory of what was necessary to construct the good citizen. "The second necessity", he said, "is decency of surroundings: including a) good lodging: b) ample space; and c) general order and beauty." For Morris, the provision of decent living arrangements was second only to the right to work as a necessity for a functioning society. However, there was no sense that he was advocating a bare minimum provision for working classes suffering the squalor of Victorian London. He went on: "Order and beauty means that not only our houses must be stoutly and properly built, but also that they be ornamented duly." To build a house without ornament and decoration was, for Morris, socially negligent. It is ironic that Morris's wallpapers have become so bound up with bourgeois interior design when, in fact, his was one of the most radical of Socialist agendas.

The next time that architecture and design were so overtly linked to social goals was with the rise of Modernism, the beginnings of which were intimately bound up with a change of attitude about the domestic interior. Such designers as Le Corbusier, Eileen Gray, Pierre Chareau, Charlotte Perriand and Robert Mallet-Stevens were influential Modernist thinkers, but all began their careers creating furniture and interiors for a wealthy clientele.

Many of London's finest practitioners make a living doing small-scale domestic work, and this is an area of incredible invention and innovation, often using meagre budgets. Many of the interiors published in the residential section of this book are small works by young architects who will go on to complete much larger projects in the near future. It is often in this impoverished context that ideas are forged which become consistent themes throughout the career of a designer. For example, 6a Architects' small fit-out for a record collector's house in north London (see pages 188–89) used ideas that found much larger expression in their shop for fashion retailer Oki-Ni (see pages 90–91). In both projects, timber is used to make a discrete skin inside an existing building, concealing services and storage and providing new spatial configurations within limited means.

Domestic work can be a trap for young architects. With limited opportunities to build at a larger scale, young talent in this country often gets stuck designing domestic interiors for wealthy clients rather than moving on to larger-scale projects with a more public dimension. But in the meantime, the ideas at work here are radically changing our view of what is possible in a domestic interior. Some are challenging relatively dull developer-built residential buildings and filling them with exuberantly eclectic elements, such as Richard Hywel Evans's playful Beck penthouse (see pages 158–59). Sited in an unremarkable residential building in Docklands, it constitutes a fantasy pad for the client, exhibiting Barbarella-style forms mixed with a loft aesthetic. At the other end of the scale are projects inhabiting buildings of existing architectural value, such as Simon Conder's wonderful treatment of an ex-industrial building in Shepherdess Walk in Shoreditch (see pages 190–91), where the existing fabric of the building is not touched, but occupied by free-standing and movable elements in plywood. This project also recognizes a certain attitude to housing in London, which sees industrial spaces such as this swiftly change hands from the artists who inhabit them in semi-derelict states to wealthier owners looking to buy into the cool aura of such areas as Shoreditch.

The temporary nature that characterizes loft living is in contrast to some of the projects here that try to reinvent the archetypal housing of London. DRDH Architects' beautiful reworking of a house in Islington provides a model of how the classic Georgian house could be remade as a contemporary studio/residential building (see pages 172–73). Likewise, Tony Fretton and artist Mark Pimlott have challenged the staid Edwardiana of Chelsea with exuberant and playful interiors for large rooms, recalling Italian palazzi as much as they reference the architectural proportions of indigenous house types. The Red House in Chelsea, completed in 2003 (see pages 164–65), is one of the most eccentric and remarkable private residences built in the city in recent years, and Pimlott's interiors are artworks as much as they are decorative designs.

London has plenty of world-famous architects and designers, but perhaps lacks some of the eccentric characters of other countries – such as Dutch design collective Droog, with their satirical, conceptual art-influenced furniture and interiors, or Joep van Lieshout, with his art/furniture/interior design crossover. We also have few hubristic characters to lead the scene, such as Egypt-born US-based superstar designer Karim Rashid (who is about to design the interior of a new hotel in Brighton), or Italy's Fabio Novembre, who has recently created extraordinary interiors for tile manufacturer Bisazza in New York and Berlin.

London's role, though, is not just to support a handful of stars, but to be a crossroads for ideas and a crucible for interdisciplinary work. Some of the greatest architects – young and old – in the world are in this city, and many of them are working on a range of interiors that will come to be seen as future classics. The extreme commercial climate of London forces many to express big ideas on a small scale, such as Florian Beigel's flat in Hampstead (see pages 156–57), which translates his ideas about large-scale urban planning into a method for making a small residence. The results are beautiful. And with much young talent on show, London is guaranteed great internal environments for years to come. The challenge now is to take the attitude of the private patrons of design (and of many of the projects in this book), and apply it to municipal buildings for better-designed schools, hospitals, town halls and sports centres.

Eating, drinking and sleeping

Baltic restaurant and bar, Southwark, SE1
Seth Stein Architects/Drury Browne Architects

Baltic, a new restaurant in Southwark, might serve a fancy version of Polish peasant food, but there's nothing meagre about the spartan contemporariness of its interior design. Seth Stein, who collaborated with Drury Browne Architects on the job, is a self-styled 'post-minimalist' architect, who, after spending his early career with high-tech luminaries Norman Foster and Richard Rogers, forged a reputation in the 1990s as an achingly cool designer of domestic interiors, evidenced by his hugely well-publicized restoration of the top floor of a Lutyens building, 68 Pall Mall.

He has since diversified into commercial interiors, including shops for the Whistles fashion chain, and into art exhibition spaces. Baltic is his first restaurant, and occupies a very difficult site that had previously been an agglomeration of backlands warehouses and garages behind the façade of a domestic Georgian terrace.

The shape of the plan meant that a pinch-point halfway in was inevitable, beyond which it opens out into the back warehouse area, now stripped and housing the main dining room. This problem has not really been solved, with an unsatisfying space used for tables and cash-register points occupying the hinge point between the bar and the main restaurant. However, the architect has been able to create two environments with very different atmospheres. The bar area is darker, with an industrial aesthetic suggested by the existing steel columns and the lacquered steel bar tempered by timber-lined walls. The restaurant is high and lit from skylights, the historic structure stripped back to its bare form and showing off reconditioned timber trusses.

The materials are rich, particularly the carefully chosen elements in amber, such as one fascia of the bar and the delicate amber mobile hanging from the restaurant ceiling. Despite a certain incoherence and lack of character, particularly when the bar is full, there is enough here to suggest that Stein's career will go on to greater things.

Cafeteria restaurant, Ladbroke Grove, W10
Wells Mackereth

The early work of young architects is a fragile thing. Starting small-scale commercial work can mean that many jobs are demolished or unrecognizably altered within a couple of years of completion. Your early masterpiece is then in the hands of possibly unsympathetic designers, also eager to make their mark.

Cafeteria is not this building's first incarnation as a restaurant – it was briefly the epitome of cool London dining as Belgo, which had been designed by Foreign Office Architects. Roaringly popular for a couple of years, Belgo was closed in 2001 when John Torode, the proprietor of Smiths of Smithfield (see pages 56–57), took it over to turn it into what has become Cafeteria. Wells Mackereth, the architects behind Smiths, had to wrestle with the iconic architecture of the Foreign Office Architects-designed vaults while putting an identifiable stamp on the space for the new owners.

The refit has displayed a very different approach from the *bierkeller* feel of Belgo. The principal interventions are pieces conceived as 'giant furniture', designed to improve acoustics, break up the space and provide some intimacy. Amorphous duck-egg blue mdf structures, designed and built by furniture company Benchmark in collaboration with Wells Mackereth, were placed around the space and upholstered to provide seating. They also accommodate waiter stations on the outside, and a new bar runs down one side of the room.

The first-floor mezzanine used to overlook the main space. Now it accommodates a chic cocktail bar, allowing glimpses of the restaurant area through shuttered windows rather than revealing the entire volume. Other touches include Eames chairs with Eiffel bases – enhancing the upmarket cafeteria atmosphere – and strangely retro fibreglass lampshades by Dutch firm Moooi. If you saw the space before, this new fit-out will feel slightly like a compromised version of the original, and it is not quite in the league of Wells Mackereth's Smiths of Smithfield interior. For most, though, it will work well.

The Cinnamon Club private members' bar, Westminster, SW1
Mueller Mueller Kneer Associates

When it comes to the interior design of Indian restaurants, we have only just left behind the days of flock wallpaper, gilt furniture and all manner of chintz on mahogany bar tops. There is something utterly charming about that mix, though – seeing two cultures' ideas of luxury collide.

The Cinnamon Club is no ordinary Indian restaurant, however. Numbering a host of celebrities among its regulars, the restaurant produces some of the finest Indian cuisine outside Rajasthan. The Club occupies the old Westminster Library, which was sold off by the council in 1997, and retains the Victorian municipal grandeur and an environment that is still strongly library-like: books still line the walls, and parquet floors and original screens continue to dominate.

When the club decided to build a new basement bar for members, it forsook its Victorian heritage and embraced an opulent and intimate contemporary aesthetic. Fabrics hanging from the wall are neutral enough, but the organic modern forms of the archway links between spaces and the choreographed lighting suggest something much more sensuous. The dominant feature of the bar area is a floor-to-ceiling glass projection screen, which can show one single image that functions as live wallpaper, or specially commissioned video works. On the bar's opening night, Indian musician Talvin Singh appeared on the screen in a live video linkup with Delhi.

The furniture consists mainly of contemporary leather banquettes and chairs, with more traditional tables made from the rare Indian wood seesham, which changes colour with the seasons. The cocktail bar also catches the eye; made entirely from bonded glass and lit from within, it continues the theme of indirect lighting that permeates the space.

In short, the Cinnamon Club is intimate and yet totally unafraid of luxury. This may only be a few miles west, but it feels leagues away from Brick Lane.

Crussh bar, Cornhill, EC3
Richard Hywel Evans Architecture and Design

Richard Hywel Evans's role at Crussh, a juice bar in the City, extended far beyond the ordinary realm of the architect. His practice chose and co-ordinated all members of the design team, including graphics and branding consultants, meaning that the distinctive interior identity they created would complement Crussh's wider branding and could be rolled out across other stores planned for the future.

Hywel Evans's original scheme for the shop fell foul of the somewhat conservative planning policy in the City (the tiny shop is part of a Grade 2 listed building). The plan had been to create a double-skinned façade, lit from behind, where passers-by could watch juice bubble between the glass layers. The final result was scaled back somewhat, but is still full of flair. Behind the purple shop front are psychedelic graphics and a multicoloured counter. An American-walnut counter faces the street, and a calmer area towards the back of the floorplate contains more relaxed seating in colours that form a visual patchwork of red, green, blue and yellow leather.

Hywel Evans has a flair for creating playful forms and Crussh is no exception. From the ceiling hang various amoeboid structures, hand-carved from styrofoam and accommodating lighting and projection systems. These refer to the equally amorphous shapes of the fittings and furniture throughout the bar. These curvy forms are supposed to reflect the unthreatening and healthy wares on sale at Crussh, which try to provide an alternative to the fast food dominating the market. Whether Hywel Evans succeeds in taking the analogy this far is not clear, but the project certainly creates a distinctive visual identity that has now been extended to shops in Mayfair, Fleet Street and Canary Wharf.

Eurostar lounge, Waterloo station, SE1
Philippe Starck

There are two big problems with Nicholas Grimshaw's spectacular Waterloo International Eurostar terminal, and both of them concern the interior. One is that the progression from check-in desk to train is arranged so that you only get to see the underside of the magnificent train shed for a few seconds before boarding the train. The second is that the spaces you do get to inhabit while excitedly waiting for your train to Paris or Brussels are like the worst thought-out airport lounges, especially for economy travellers – rows of seats with the odd kiosk selling egg mayonnaise sandwiches.

Although Eurostar is a fantastic way to cross the Channel, it was in dire need of a makeover, and what better man to do it than that cheekily ubiquitous Gallic style guru, Philippe Starck. Starck took on the task of completely rebranding the train service, a £35,000,000 job that included new first and business class lounges at Waterloo, Brussels-Midi and Paris Gare du Nord stations. Endearing himself immediately to the British public, Starck claimed that people should, for a start, dress better when they boarded the trains: "There is a tendency today for people to travel wearing purple jogging bottoms, green fluorescent sweaters and orange Nike trainers," he told *The Times* newspaper. "I can understand that people want to be comfortable, but it is possible to be elegant as well."

From this he went on to create a wilfully eclectic lounge in the bowels of the Grimshaw building, which can accommodate 120 passengers, with a smaller lounge for 60 passengers opening as part of a later phase. Trademark Starck touches, such as camp chandeliers and marble bar tops, sit next to comfortable loungers providing space for business travellers to work or relax. Passengers can even take a massage in one of the automatic massage chairs screened off at one end of the lounge. Toilet doors are marked not with conventional male and female signs, but with razors and lipsticks. It's very nice indeed – but you can only get in if you have a top-price ticket.

Starck has created a fun beginning to a project that will eventually see all train interiors upgraded, too. One hopes that some of the rebranding will be aimed at providing a better travelling experience for the tracksuit-wearing public, as well as for premium-ticket holders.

Eyre Brothers restaurant, Shoreditch, EC2
Waugh Thistleton

Eyre Brothers is the first restaurant to be run by the chefs responsible for The Eagle, the cult gastropub at the forefront of the high-quality pub food resurgence now gripping the capital's dining culture. And if there is a sense of chefs in top gastropubs slumming it somewhat, Robert and David Eyre chose Shoreditch – the capital of elegant slumming – as the place to unleash their restaurant concept on the world. Given this background, the restaurant, designed by Shoreditch-based Waugh Thistleton, is not what you might expect. The interior is immaculate and, despite the fact that it occupies a rather good 1960s concrete-frame print works, there is a feeling of classic luxury about it, suggestive more of a gentleman's club than a warehouse apartment.

Waugh Thistleton was architect for the refit of the whole building, which consists of apartments in a new extension on the top floors, commercial office space on the first floor, and the restaurant on the ground floor. The service areas of the restaurant are immaculately clean, with stainless steel and white glass surfaces lit brightly and functionally. The dining area is decked out, by contrast, in rich hardwoods, leather banquette seating, bronze and coloured glass. Its main feature is the Jotoba hardwood piece that wraps around and over the dining area, conceived not as a screen but as a kind of proscenium arch, turning the scurrying waiters and elegant diners into a piece of theatre. A 20 m (66 ft) long bar leading into the open kitchen means that the atmosphere retains something of a pub-like feel – appropriate in an area such as Shoreditch, where bars, restaurants and clubs can often be found occupying the same space.

It is one of the more polite social environments in this part of London, but the expressed polarity between the production of food and its consumption does make it a cut above most of the restaurants and bars that have spread across East London.

Grand Central bar, Great Eastern Street, Shoreditch, EC2
Block Architecture

Restaurateur and bar owner Eric Yu practically wrote the book on commissioning young designers on the up to create hip and cutting-edge drinking and dining venues. His Breakfast Group chain owns Opium Bar, Soho, designed by Paris-based Miguel Cancio Martins; The Social in Little Portland Street, one of the first projects of white-hot London architect David Adjaye; and now Grand Central in Shoreditch, designed by the hotly tipped Block Architecture.

Block is also responsible for the slightly more polite Market Place bar (see page 46), around the corner from Adjaye's The Social, but Grand Central is its *tour de force* so far. Graeme Williamson and Zoë Smith, partners in the practice, have created an interior inspired by the busy roads outside the bar, integrating a number of dynamic visual elements into the stripped-back bones of an old bank building in London's achingly trendy Shoreditch triangle.

Williamson says that he sees bar design as a very specific task, and one that relies as much on the ephemeral as on such architectural principles as commodity, firmness and delight. "Bars are a different breed. By their nature they have to be new, and there's a sense of impermanence," he says. Thus, their scheme at Grand Central touches the existing fabric of the building lightly, retaining an ambience of the old that has become characteristic of interiors in the area.

The most striking aspect of the project is the lighting. Inspired by long-exposure photography, Block created a bar fascia made of stacked live-edge Perspex, lit from behind. The red streaks call to mind the cars racing by outside. On the ceiling, galvanized metal lighting conduits wind their way from the entrance through the space in a way that accentuates movement and mobility, while bare bulbs hanging from them contribute an industrial aesthetic. This dramatic insertion has since been compromised by the addition of other ceiling-hung lighting, but the effect is still impressive.

Tiled patterns also play their part – the full-height bottle gallery behind the bar has an undulating, repeating pattern that disorientates the visitor and emphasizes the scale of the building. Downstairs, white glazed bricks (in Dutch proportions) are used in the passageway to the toilets, creating an atmosphere at once antiseptic and subterranean.

Williamson and Smith clearly have talents that will lead to much larger building projects (their recent refurbishment of the Museum of Modern Art in Oxford is testament to that), but their bar and restaurant interiors will continue to delight for a while longer. Their next bar project, occupying an old butcher's shop in Clerkenwell, will use a variety of innovative materials, such as resin-coated plywood reminiscent of the mahogany-lined walls of gentlemen's clubs, and a bar surface made of rosa aurora marble lit from below. Their touch with materials is reminiscent of David Adjaye: never bound to fashion, but always innovative and deeply cool. Grand Central is another hit in an area already full of decent contemporary bar and restaurant design.

Hakkasan, Hanway Street, W1
Christian Liaigre/Jestico & Whiles

Christian Liaigre is one of France's most influential designers, designing bestselling furniture for manufacturers such as Poliform and diversifying very convincingly into interiors both in his own country and abroad. One of his big breakthroughs was to design New York's hip Mercer hotel and kitchen in 1997, which propelled him into the big league of interior designers internationally.

He has completed two restaurant interiors in London: the enduringly popular Busaba Eathai on Poland Street in Soho and Hakkasan, a smart oriental fusion restaurant that has been at, or near, the top of London's fashionable dining scene for some time. Busaba is, along with Wagamama, the *sine qua non* of chic canteen eating. Hakkasan is more upmarket and much more expensive, and so had to deal with a more conventional table layout. The location is also inauspicious – a dank and deeply unattractive alleyway running between Oxford Street and Tottenham Court Road. To cap it all, the site is a basement.

Liaigre, working with architecture practice Jestico & Whiles, decided to make the space as fashionably removed from this context as possible. A slate-clad staircase, studded with red lights, leads down from the street. The space is dark and divided by ornate lacquered marquetry screens set against bright blue walls. This gives most areas of the restaurant a pleasing intimacy.

Hakkasan is conceived more as a holistic venue than a simple restaurant, so there is a bar 16 m (53 ft) long and blue leather seating suggesting bar or club as much as restaurant. A high-end sound system also means that the space can be acoustically tailored to allow for quiet conversationalists or enthusiastic clubbers.

At nearly £3,000,000, this is one of the most expensive restaurant interiors in London, and it is easy to see where the money has gone. The staff are starchy, but it's one of the most spectacular places to eat in the city.

Innecto restaurant, Baker Street, NW1
Jestico & Whiles

Jestico & Whiles is an architecture practice that has a somewhat patchy record in its work, which ranges from very ordinary commercial architecture to some very stylish interiors indeed. Innecto is one project that the critics seemed to agree on, winning a host of awards for its arresting interior.

Innecto's shop front is formed of pivoting panels 4 m (13 ft) high made of burnished steel and amber glass, which can be opened fully to the street. Inside, the restaurant has space for 110 covers, with a cocktail bar in the basement.

The main restaurant is 25 m (82 ft) deep with 4.5 m (15 ft) ceilings, the concrete shell semi-shielded by dramatic arches of overlapping strips of American black walnut. Visible through the gaps in this woven fabric is the original concrete, painted orange and lit obliquely to accentuate the texture. These lights also wash the floor under banquettes of solid walnut, which appear to hover as unsupported planes. A servery of backlit yellow glass reveals the open-hearth oven and the distant movement of the chefs. Off the main restaurant a more intimate cave of polished plaster defines a smaller dining area.

The walls and floor of the reception and pre-dining area are lined with honed limestone with an elliptical staircase to the basement punched through. The main staircase, clad in raw steel sheet, leads to the subterranean cocktail bar. Here, a curving plaster wall creates a tapering drum, with bench seating of heavy coach hide. Again, the wall stops short of the ceiling, allowing glimpses of the illuminated raw concrete shell.

Innecto won the *Design Week* Best Restaurant Design in 2001 and *Theme* magazine's Best Restaurant Interior Design award in 2002, garnering wide publicity and giving the owner, restaurateur Sami Wasif, excellent return for the £670,000 contract.

The Light, Shoreditch, EC1
Waugh Thistleton

This spectacular building, which sits on the very border between the business heart of London and the poor borough of Hackney, is a spectacular piece of industrial heritage that was nearly demolished shortly before it was purchased and turned into the popular bar it now is. It was London's first and only remaining purpose-built electricity power station, and is Grade 1 listed.

Because of its location, on the edge of Broadgate (the extensive office development that has grown up around Liverpool Street), there was a ready-made clientele. Owing to heritage restrictions and the sensitivity of the architects, this has become one of the best bar interiors in the area. The interventions are minimal, and much of the £750,000 budget was spent on making good the existing fabric. Brickwork was cleaned inside and out and exterior stonework restored. Some parts of the building were lost or beyond repair, and replacements and new interventions are identifiably contemporary.

The Light consists of a ground-floor bar and restaurant with a members' bar on the first floor and washrooms on a mezzanine level. A section of original floor was removed to create a triple-height space – 9m (30 ft) from floor to ceiling – on one side of the bar, which makes it very theatrical. From every point one seems to have a perspective on somewhere else – a perfect attribute for a bar catering to the wealthy, see-and-be-seen-obsessed City workers.

The lighting is perhaps the most impressive and obvious of the architect's interventions. Made simply from wire and bare bulbs, some lamps are arranged as minimal chandeliers, and others hang as single lights. Upstairs is much more conventional, with ordinary leather couches and the exposed beams of the original roof. The bar has proven very popular indeed – perhaps too popular for its own good – but the tough nature of the conversion has meant that the building still looks splendid, even on a sweaty Friday night.

Market Place, W1
Block Architecture

It is fair to say that the architecture and design scene in London was waiting with bated breath to see how Block Architecture would follow up its incredible interior at Grand Central in Shoreditch (see pages 38–39). The practice itself, not wanting to be typecast as bar designers, decided to do something much more modest than the spectacle of Grand Central, and Market Place is probably the more welcoming of the two bars.

The client, Canteloupe Group, had a record of good taste in interior decoration, as evidenced by the raw and atmospheric interior of its home restaurant, Canteloupe, and by its more recent Cargo nightclub designed by Jamie Fobert – both of which are in Shoreditch. Canteloupe's move into the West End meant that the kind of designs acceptable in Shoreditch might have to be tempered, despite the fact that the site is just around the corner from the raw concrete of David Adjaye's Social bar.

Market Place is intended as a reinterpretation of the traditional pub, described by partner Graeme Williamson as "an environment that is exclusively unexclusive". The architects took as their inspiration not the dark painted timber of the London pub, but the rough-sawn Douglas fir of the Swiss chalet to give a sense of escapism and a feeling of a rural retreat from the urban setting outside. Humorous touches include artificial grass areas in the lobby and stairwell to enforce further the idea of a country hideaway. Furniture for the bar is also in solid Douglas fir and was designed loosely around the classic picnic table. Timber is overwhelmingly the material of choice, and the atmosphere within is none the worse for it.

Downstairs is a more nightclub-like atmosphere, with alcoves that hint at the form of the original cellar and provide crannies in which to hide yourself away.

In all, and despite its modest scale, this is a great space that provides respite from the West End hustle and bustle.

Public Life bar, Commercial Street, Spitalfields, E1
Mueller Kneer Associates

Mueller Kneer Associates is a young architecture practice based in Clerkenwell. Headed by two German partners, they have recently come to prominence in the style press for a series of bars and restaurants of consummate style. They have tackled some inauspicious sites in their time, but creating a bar in a subterranean public lavatory, just 65 sq m (700 sq ft) and without any windows, takes the biscuit. The public loo is between two of east London's most imposing landmarks – Nicholas Hawksmoor's Christ Church and the historic Spitalfields market – in an area undergoing rapid gentrification with the advance of City offices eastwards.

Public Life, although small, is conceived as a crucible, mixing the various social groups that swarm around this area, equidistant as it is between Brick Lane's Banglatown and the offices of Broadgate. The public convenience was built in the nineteenth century, and since there were many original details still extant, the major interventions were kept to a minimum, revealing black-and-white Victorian floor tiles, glazed wall tiles and cast-iron railings in the process.

These are complemented with contemporary materials, most obviously signalled from the street by the new glazed entrance box, which is the only sign above ground that anything lies below the pavement. In the summer, outside seating augments this minimal intrusion.

Descent into the bar is by way of a new open-tread concrete staircase, inset with glass 'lenses' that allow light into the depths of the basement space. The stairway provides a two-pace descent, changing pace halfway down and adding a processional excitement to the journey. The entire ceiling is made from the same concrete as the stairway, inset with glass, meaning that the space is very well lit during the day, despite having no conventional glazed openings. At night, this effect is reversed, with light shining up through the pavement from the bar below.

The project was developed with film-maker Neil Bell and the client, Strike Foundation – an art organization with a strong situationist influence that focuses on the potential of mass media in art. The interior is therefore often occupied by people tapping away sagely at computers and creating the latest audio-visual installation.

Public Life is unique and is a blessed relief from the over-designed bars that have broken out like a rash elsewhere in Shoreditch.

Restaurant at the Royal Albert Hall, Kensington, SW7
Softroom

Softroom is a young architectural practice that made its name early on with a series of computer-generated landscapes and environments for television, music videos and magazines such as *Wallpaper*. Even their early buildings – which included the remarkable Kielder belvedere in Northumberland with its mirrored steel exterior – resembled computer fantasies.

With their new restaurant for the Royal Albert Hall, Softroom delved into the Establishment, and combined old-school elegance with a touch of bold geometry.

The scheme's most striking feature is the 25 m (82 ft) helix of tensioned wire running through the restaurant, which holds small discs of reflective steel that redirect light around the room from spotlights concealed in the wall. The helix is intended to draw the visitor through the restaurant, which is a linear, curved space that could easily have become a corridor in the wrong hands. It also means that space is transformed in the evening, as patches of light reflect around the room and strange shadows are cast on the ceiling. The passage of time is given a physical presence and makes the atmosphere of the building particularly special in the evening, which seems appropriate for a concert hall.

Despite the grandeur of the building in which they sit, the dining rooms did not have much Victorian detail to reveal. As well as restoring their original proportions, the architect has tried to accentuate what was there, including terracotta surrounds on the windows that previously had been concealed behind heavy curtains.

The other materials recall the luxury and opulence of the main hall but viewed through a contemporary lens. The red velvet wall and bench seat, inlaid with mirrored panels, is the most obvious example of this, but also the white Corian bar standing in front of a black walnut wall, and the use of mirrored planters placed by the curving wall.

6 St Chad's Place, WC1
Squire and Partners

Architect Michael Squire's experience in the bar and restaurant sector extends much further than simply designing them. His first venture as a bar developer – Sand in Clapham, completed in 1999 – has been very successful and gave the firm the taste for more.

Squire bought 6 St Chad's Place, a small workshop building close to his offices in the King's Cross conservation area, with a view to providing a restaurant and bar in a part of London not known as a destination for revellers. The workshop sits directly above the Thameslink train platforms. The objective was to touch the building lightly, allowing as much as possible of the original architecture to be exposed, including the spectacular timber trusses. The original brick was sand blasted, and the existing roof-light was replaced to allow natural light into the heart of the building. Two large timber doors create a generous opening on to the street, allowing for tables to be placed outside in the summer.

The bar itself is one of the most beautiful you will see in London – 9 m (30 ft) of low-level cream solid-state acrylic that provides an inviting serving area. Behind the bar, the architect created a new surface of ceramic tiles echoing the proportions of the brickwork. Colours are muted greys, blues and creams that form a backdrop to flashes of red from ashtrays and candle-holders.

The most eyecatching part of the building is the back wall, which is occupied by a huge customized photograph of a Thameslink train leaving the platform. This adds drama to one's experience of the interior and reminds the visitor of the train tracks beneath. The image is printed on wallpaper and can be changed easily. The £316,000 budget also stretched to furnishing the bar with classic Eames chairs and original 1950s Danish sofas.

Silka restaurant, Borough Market, SE1
Mueller Kneer Associates

Marianne Mueller and Olaf Kneer have impeccable architectural credentials: Mueller has worked with noted Dutch academic Raoul Bunschoten, and Kneer performed a stint with British architect Ian Ritchie, working on his Leipzig Glass Hall. Their practice was started in 1997 and they quickly developed a specialization in sensuous bar and restaurant interiors.

Silka is one of the most recent of these. It is a restaurant that serves "energy food from the ayurvedic tradition", which incorporates food preparation into a lifestyle that includes yoga and controlled breathing. The interior tries to reflect this holism through horizontal layers of internal finishes, and huge white discs float on the ceiling like abstract clouds. There is a mixture of cream and red rendered surfaces augmented with rich exotic hardwoods, including Indian rosewood, ebony and makore, which are backlit to create an illusion of depth.

Indirect light comes from behind the wall cladding, the cloud ceiling, and frames surrounding the two openings to the bar and restaurant area. These frames are main light sources and also function as guides from the street into the restaurant. The frame around the bar signals arrival in the space, and the kitchen is flagged by another of these light boxes, which recall Art Deco styling in the way that frosted glass is held in rectangular steel frames.

The space is intended to be "an antidote to London's hectic life", according to the architects, and this demure scheme certainly realizes that aim. However, there is something distinctly urbane about the mix of rich woods and neutral colours that belies its somewhat mystical inspirations.

Sketch, Mayfair, W1
The Manser Practice/Mourad Mazouz/
Noé Duchaufour-Lawrance/Gabhan O'Keefe

Per square metre, Sketch may be the most expensive project in this book. This extraordinarily flamboyant fit-out of a 1779 townhouse on Conduit Street cost £10,500,000 to achieve, and has produced one of London's most exclusive – and notoriously expensive – dining rooms.

The restaurant (which also contains two bars, a nightclub, a gallery and a pâtisserie) is the brainchild of restaurateur Mourad Mazouz, who employed the then 25-year-old French interior designer Noé Duchaufour-Lawrance to design the interior and co-ordinate an all-star cast of designers to contribute various elements to the 650 sq m (7000 sq ft) space. The reception desk and entrance hall is by Ron Arad, the chandelier by Marc Newsom, there are laser sculptures by Chris Levine, a staircase by Mahbs Yaqub and furniture throughout by Jurgen Bey of Dutch design collective Droog. It is almost as if the diversity of star designers was meant to mock the building's previous use as a home of the Royal Institute of British Architects.

Among the most innovative of the installations are the twelve toilet pods, which consist of white-lacquered fibreglass egg shapes (made by a boatmaker) suspended above the West Bar, and it is these that demonstrate one of the central concepts of the project. The expression of all the elements is consciously separate from the already elaborate eighteeenth-century interior, and they read as sculptural contemporary elements rather than a coherent new skin for the building.

The two bars are perhaps where the effect is felt best. In the West Bar, white terrazzo flooring, Saarinen chairs and laser projections on the wall give a certain retro-futurist feel. The small East Bar sits within a huge plastered egg, wrapped with a grand double staircase, continuing the Barbarella aesthetic.

The sheer playfulness of Sketch is overwhelming for some, but there is little doubt that, approached in the right spirit, the interior is tremendous fun – a maximalist classic.

Smiths of Smithfield, EC1
Wells Mackereth

Smiths of Smithfield may be a relative newcomer to the restaurant scene around Clerkenwell, but it can now be said to have defined a genre. It is the epitome of found-space eating.

Smiths is set within an old listed meat warehouse that originally served the market opposite. It has been transformed to provide 1400 sq m (15,000 sq ft) of bars and dining rooms, including a new top storey of steel and glass and a terrace providing spectacular views over London.

By and large, the building has been left as far as possible to express its original structure. One is supposed to feel as if the butchers have moved out and the chefs just moved in. On the ground level, with its very generous ceiling height, is a smart and uncompromised industrial space with sensitive contemporary interventions. A 10 m (33 ft) stainless steel bar faces the entrance and joins at right angles with the food bar. This orthogonal definition still reads as temporary, but does help to give a more human scale to the room. Oak refectory tables and battered settees continue the high-class thrift-store feel, and galvanized troughs on the ceiling contain adaptable lighting systems. The floor looks like a cross between the scrubbed floor of a butcher's shop and a pavement, with an ingenious sand-rubbed asphalt flooring used liberally.

Upstairs are areas with quite different atmospheres, such as the smaller cocktail bar, with its red-lacquered fittings and booth seating. This is overlooked by a dining area above, seen through a large square opening in the floor slab. The top dining area is much more expensive than the rest, and this seems to have had a negative effect on the décor, which reverts to a more generic beige – cool but polite.

This is not a radical piece of architecture by any means, but it defines a certain lifestyle that exists in this part of London. Busy all day and serving breakfast to clubbers from 7 am, Smiths is quintessentially of its time. The interior, along with the chunky supergraphic signage, is a reflection of a specific moment in the social history of the city.

Soba restaurant, Soho Street, W1
JAS Architects

The noodle restaurant has become a genre all its own, usually implying a vaguely minimalist interior to encourage a Zen-like stoicism in the face of paying a fortune for sometimes quite minimal portions. Architect Juan Salgado's version of this aesthetic – at the very reasonably priced Soba restaurant on Soho Street – is one of the best, taking the reductive calm of Wagamama and adding a certain theatricality and urban intention.

The restaurant is situated in an old and very grand post office and incorporates many features from its heritage as a Neo-classical/Art Deco building. A row of columns still stands outside, for example, and inside, Salgado elected to retain the ornate ceiling. He cleared away some of its classical details, and has hung new elements in the space to temper the rather grandiose height. Cork-clad floating panels incorporate lighting and add to the intimacy of the restaurant.

Salgado has also kept an awkward stepped section, which was intended to demarcate private areas in the former public building. Other finishes and pieces of furniture help to defuse the institutional feel of the original. Table and bench tops are finished in bands of mahogany, and the floor is finished in slate tiles: grey in the seating areas, with a single red strip showing the circulation routes.

The dominant visual element is also the one that gives the restaurant a striking presence on the street. A screen of cork-clad poles, fixed to the back wall at varying intervals, reflects light from uplighters and complements the measured rhythm of the stone-clad columns on the exterior. For the casual passer-by, the space of the street seems to extend into the depth of the restaurant thanks to this expressive back wall.

West Street Hotel, Covent Garden, WC2
Wells Mackereth

Although an established concept in cities such as New York, boutique hotels are a relatively new thing to London. In the past decade there has been a mini-explosion of venues catering to a younger, urbane and more style-conscious traveller, who wanted contemporary design to replace the increasingly tired clichés of Kensington hotel land. While US hotelier Ian Schrager's St Martin's Lane and the Philippe Starck-designed Sanderson blazed a trail, the West Street Hotel, established by hotelier Chris Bodker, chef Rowley Leigh and Marian Scrutton, was not far behind.

The design, by Wells Mackereth, was chosen through a limited architectural competition, and the result of their work was keenly awaited by style and architectural press alike. The result did not disappoint, but was probably quieter and more dignified than some had anticipated. Guests enter the hotel through a glass façade and walk across a bridge to the reception desk, catching glimpses through the triple-height space cut through the existing six-storey building.

Within, there are two different restaurants, a basement bar and a number of different bedrooms. The most special of these are the three exclusive rooms at the top of the hotel: the Stone Room, the White Room and the Loft. The Stone Room has neutral leather sofas, brown velvet curtains and an immense roof terrace embellished with awnings. The White Room has floor-to-ceiling Carrara marble with white curtains and red leather sofas. The Loft is the *pièce de résistance* – one of the finest contemporary hotel spaces in London. It is a huge, vaulted room, with stained oak floors and floor-to-ceiling windows. One wall, clad entirely in green slate, has an open fireplace, and fake fur throws and tulip chairs finish the look of this luxury bolthole. The bar in the basement is also tastefully contemporary, with honed granite surfaces, leather banquettes and walls, and subtle artwork.

Zimzun restaurant, Fulham Broadway shopping centre, SW6
Tilney Shane

A location within which it is almost impossible to find good design is the shopping centre. Zimzun, a new oriental restaurant (to be the first of a chain) in Fulham Broadway shopping centre, bucks this trend. It is one of the best works by the interior design and graphics consultancy Tilney Shane, which has carried out work for a range of clients from Little Chef to the BBC, but has rarely made the pulse race.

At Zimzun, the brainchild of restaurant entrepreneur Peter Ponnampalan, the practice was given free range to work on everything from the chopsticks to the interior of the restaurant, including its graphic identity.

Teak furniture and sandstone floors set a tone of material luxury, not typical of chain restaurants in shopping malls. Low-level canteen-style tables incorporate glass tanks with floating water lilies that cast rippled reflections onto the ceiling, catching the light from droplet light-fittings that hover above. These fittings are made from 600 strands of opalescent beads and hang from a soffit concealing lighting. The effect is excellent, casting slim rays of light across the restaurant.

There is a strong obsession with geometric shapes, from the candle-lit mosaic-tiled niches to the box shelving behind the bar, which accommodates individual bottles. The graphic identity is also compelling, with a purple livery and American-style cardboard cartons for those taking food away.

The building is not particularly original, borrowing from more expensive projects such as Christian Liaigre's Hakkasan (see pages 40–41) and Busaba restaurants in the West End. However, there is no shame in copying a blueprint of this quality, and it provides an individual, contemporary and sociable dining space. The highest compliment it can be paid is to say that one almost forgets about the mall atmosphere outside the door.

Zuma restaurant, Knightsbridge, SW1
Super Potato

You could probably guess from the name that Super Potato design consultancy is Japanese. Founded in 1973 by Takashi Sugimoto (the moniker comes from his own nickname), the consultancy has grown to become one of the most prolific restaurant and bar designers in south-east Asia, carrying out projects in Japan, Singapore, Korea and elsewhere. Their work is characterized by the use of natural materials, and their skills were honed on a series of restaurants for the Hyatt hotel chain, the most famous of which was their Mezza 9 restaurant in Singapore. Despite this corporate client base, the consultancy has retained a certain mystique, derived, in part, from its self-consciously kooky name and branding.

Zuma, a Japanese restaurant in the heart of Knightsbridge, is Super Potato's first project in Europe, and so feels freshly and authentically eccentric Japanese. The interior consists of a series of three counters – the Sake bar, the Robota bar and the Sushi counter – alongside a more conventional dining area. At the back are two private dining rooms screened from the rest of the space by oversized timber trellises, which give privacy without cutting the occupants off completely from the atmosphere of the main space.

Materials are what strike the visitor, and were also responsible for the super-high budget (£1,750,000). The bars are made of granite quarried, cut and shipped over from China, and topped with a length of etched glass. Furniture, including the no-expense-spared chef's table, was imported from Indonesia. In all, this is an incredibly lavish project, reflecting the clientele – Hollywood stars and the sons and daughters of media magnates – and the price of dinner, which can easily reach £150 for two people.

Zuma is eclectic and, in places, downright barmy – a small taste of interior design Tokyo-style, which has scant regard for the conventions or tasteful surfaces of Western restaurants.

Shopping

Alexander McQueen boutique, Old Bond Street, W1
William Russell

William Russell is the erstwhile partner of David Adjaye who, since the dissolution of the partnership, has become Britain's most famous young architect. Russell's career has taken a while longer to get going, but with his series of boutique interiors for one of the UK's biggest fashion names – Alexander McQueen – he has entered the big league.

The first of these stores was in New York, and the London store, on Old Bond Street in the heart of the fashion ghetto, follows this template, modulating it with a different colour palette. The New York store was resplendent in ice white with hues of green. The London store is coloured with a pink terrazzo, which retains the otherworldly feeling of the NY store, but gives it a peculiarly camp brand of glamour.

The interior is conceived as just two surfaces: the pink terrazzo floor, which rises up to form benches and seats, and the ceiling, which is clad in plaster and folds down to form sinuous walls and stalactite-like columns.

Unusually for a boutique, a high degree of craft went into its making. Butcher Plasterworks, the render contractor, constructed the complex curved forms off-site from traditional fibrous plaster – a mixture of hessian and plaster. This, with the terrazzo, gives the whole interior a certain synergy with the work of Alexander McQueen – a mix of glamour, traditional craftsmanship and process-based production.

The fit-out also demonstrates an appealing tension between luxury and simplicity: a very limited palette of materials has been used, but the form suggests opulence and glamour. Russell says: "We restrained the palette and used just three materials so we could create a sculpted but not overly detailed interior that stays neutral against the clothes." If this is neutral, it is exciting to imagine what Russell might do when he's being radical.

Aveda, Marylebone High Street, W1;
Westbourne Grove, W2; Drury Lane, WC2
Jamie Fobert Architects

Jamie Fobert, one of architecture's brightest prospects, currently luxuriates in the title of 'brand guardian' of the organic cosmetics company Aveda. His work, though, has little to do with the marketingspeak peddled by many branding experts. His buildings are elementally tectonic and materially simple, and build on an apprenticeship spent with British master David Chipperfield.

Fobert's relationship with Aveda goes back to 1997, when he was asked to come up with a project for the flagship store on Marylebone High Street. This scheme, which became a touchstone project for the practice, was developed closely with client and builder in a fast process, with the architect reacting to changes on site week by week.

The project, which became something of a template for the stores, attempts to embody in architecture some of the values of the Aveda brand, which sells rigorously organic cosmetic products, all of which can be traced to vegetable ingredients. Fobert took a simple and limited palette of materials – black steel, raw concrete and teak – and used them in chunky proportions. These solid single materials were an attempt to get away from the ephemerality of a conventional shop fit-out and to give a sense of permanence and trust to the firm's premises. Materials are rarely mixed. Fobert's aim was to avoid becoming obsessed with millimetre-perfect dimensions, and to allow a sense of relaxed imprecision.

The themes have continued into the most recent stores – an old Neo-classical bank building on Westbourne Grove, completed in 2001, and the shop in Covent Garden, which accommodates a café, retail area and hair salon, with training facilities on the glazed mezzanine floor. The palette of materials is adjusted to take into account existing conditions. For example, the Covent Garden building was already substantially finished in concrete, so further concrete interventions were kept to a minimum and the timber maximized instead.

The formula has also been applied, in miniature, to the many Aveda concessions in Selfridges, Harvey Nichols etc., which have Fobert-designed steel and timber cabinets with built-in lighting to accommodate the cosmetics ranges.

B&B Italia showroom, Brompton Road, SW3
John Pawson/Antonio Citterio

John Pawson is the man responsible for taking minimalism into the mainstream, translating it from art-historical category to lifestyle choice. He has designed many great interiors, all of which have a strongly ascetic quality – large expanses of white plastered walls with the minimum of interruptions. He has also published several books, including a recipe book, all of which criticize "the jarring distraction of possessions".

It is perhaps ironic, then, that B&B Italia, one of the most chic names in contemporary furniture, decided to put its showpiece boutique in a Pawson building, filling it with possessions from Pawson-friendly minimalist furniture to distinctly camp zebra-pattern rugs. The firm employed Italian designer Antonio Citterio to do the fit-out, and the result is a compromised, but still very impressive, space.

Pawson's building fills a very long and thin site on the Brompton Road, pushing finger-like to the backs of the surrounding houses. A curving lead roof sits above the most dramatic part of the interior – the large vault of the rear-most showroom. Citterio's fit-out is materially a little disappointing: the slate wall does not make the most of the natural light spilling down from the clerestory and reflecting up from the cream limestone on the floor. He has, however, managed to preserve the drama of the journey through the shop, with its long, shallow ramp bringing the visitor from the street into the other realm of the vault.

The mezzanine features cedar floors and natural light, providing a more homely setting for B&B's Maxalto collection, and under the mezzanine sit three Arclinea kitchens. Through the length of the main space hang seven glass sheets supporting abat-jour lights designed for Flos. Despite its highly commercial use, the space remains truly dramatic, even if it might be a little cluttered for Pawson's taste.

Bodas Bodywear, Notting Hill, W11
ACQ

Making a minimalist interior can be either an aesthetic choice or can be born out of simple economics. "Less is more" can often be translated as "less is all we can afford".

This is certainly the case at Bodas Bodywear, a new underwear shop completed in early 2002 by ACQ architects. The client, a dotcom entrepreneur looking for a high-street presence for a small underwear business, had only £30,000 to spend on fitting out a small but perfectly formed retail space in west London. One of the reasons for the tight budget was that there was a very short lease on the shop – just three years – so every part of the new interior had to be demountable.

The fit-out elements therefore stand self-consciously separate from the existing fabric of the building. The brick walls of the shop are left uncovered and are simply painted white. The York stone ceiling is left exposed, and the floor is covered in a polished concrete surface.

The interior is just 3.2 m (10.5 ft) wide by 12.5 m (41 ft) long, so the architect decided to blow up some black-and-white photographs of the product range to help scale the space. The models in the photos appear bigger than life-size, and there is the sense of being very close to a billboard, providing a shift of scale that helps to save the store from seeming too small.

Part of the Bodas philosophy is to avoid a department-store atmosphere in which every corner is crammed with products. Here, the goods are stored in specially tailored drawers that are of the exact proportions of the packaging, and only the minimum product is out on display.

ACQ has also completed a store for Bodas in Leadenhall Market that conforms to the same philosophy, but which has more the feel of a completed retail fit-out. The charm of the Notting Hill shop is in its subtle placing of elements in an existing space, and its creativity with such a small budget.

Bulthaup showroom, South Kensington, SW7
John Pawson

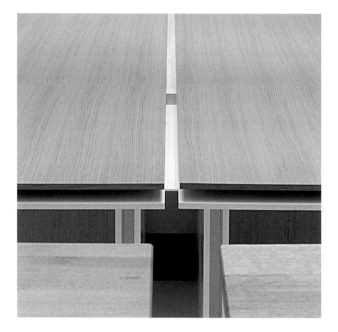

John Pawson's Bulthaup showroom has been called the "invisible store" by some – a description the designer would find exceedingly satisfying, not just because of his abiding fascination with paring down his buildings to their absolute essentials, but also because it fulfils the client's wish to have as subtle a physical presence as possible for this showroom, and to avoid overbearing product displays.

Bulthaup, suppliers of high-specification kitchens for wealthy people's houses, wanted a showroom that would not show their products, but would provide somewhere for in-depth consultation with customers a place where architects could bring their clients. The choice of site – on a low-key residential street in South Kensington – set the tone, and Pawson continued it within. The main entrance is through full-height glass doors from the street, but views inside are regulated by the different degrees of opacity that the architect has given the panels of the glass façade. The showroom itself is long and thin, with little natural light, and the products are all but hidden.

At the street entrance the space feels almost tunnel-like, but towards the back is a much higher, top-lit area. Pawson has attempted to unify these two diverse spaces by allowing views through the whole length of the interior. The stone floor also helps with this unification, and interruptions are minimized by concentrating services, computers and storage around the structural columns. There are two functioning kitchens, but the main attention is paid to the huge bespoke table for consultations.

Pawson was the ideal choice for a company that desired less to show off its products than to express a certain lifestyle it would like to be associated with. Although the store has been called invisible, it works hard to express the values of Bulthaup as a brand for the connoisseur.

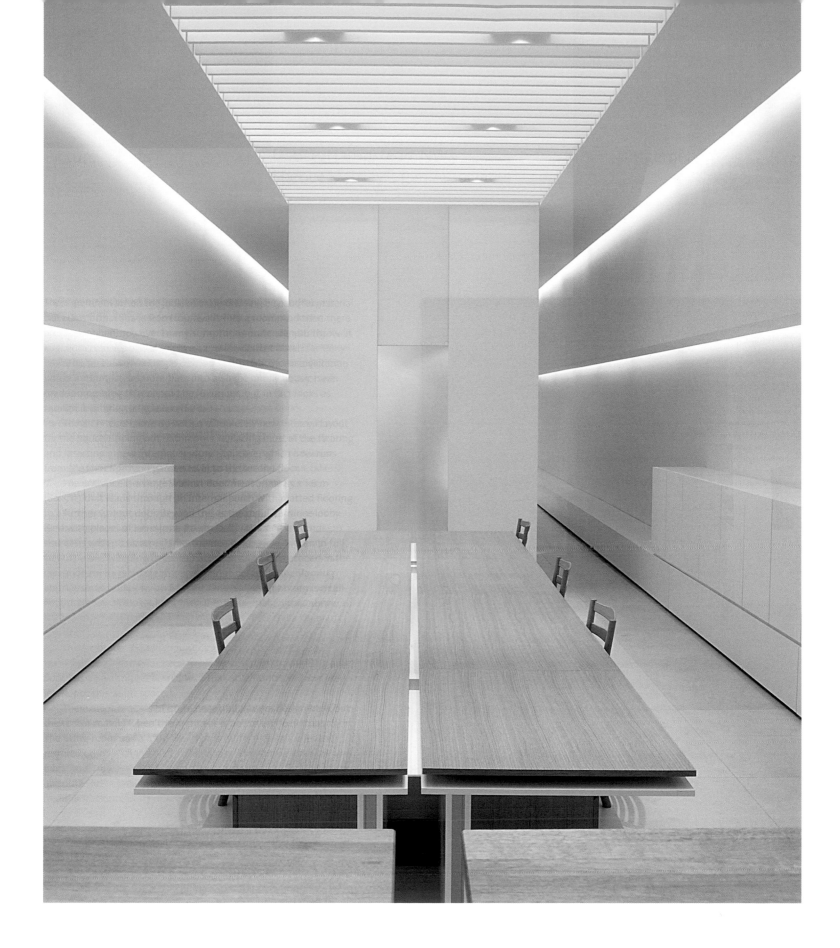

Ebony & Co., Chelsea, SW3
Softroom

A reputation for achieving high-quality architecture and interiors is not always such a desirable thing for a young practice. When many should be moving on to bigger and better things, they get caught producing the same project over and over again in order to pay the bills. Softroom has always avoided being the kind of practice that produces high numbers of bland projects, but it has attained a reputation in boutique retailing that is second to none: it has repeated its trick of stylish interiors, increasing footfall and sales in several locations.

These jobs include the reserved cool of cult knitwear designer John Smedley's stores on Brook Street and the King's Road, menswear label Designworks on Broadwick Street, and men's and women's wear departments in one of London's most prestigious department stores, Selfridges. Ebony & Co. is not your normal retailer. The Chelsea-based firm supplies high-specification timber flooring to the rich home-owners of the area, and it needed a base where visitors could compare different grains, colours and veneers.

Softroom conceived of a gallery-like atmosphere with large squares of timber hung on the walls, turning surfaces into objects. This could be read either as a witty comment on the nature of art and consumerism, or simply as a way to give the product on sale the status of high culture. Softroom used wide boards throughout, making the link between the size of a tree and the cut dimensions of the planks. Again, this might have a double meaning – an oblique reference to Ebony & Co.'s parent company, which is called Wide Plank. The walls are decorated with a band of backlit glass squares that reflect the dark timber floor. Another nice touch is the alternating colours of the columns painted in varying shades, accentuating the structural grid of the building.

Although Ebony & Co. was completed with an extremely low budget, attention to detail makes it a classy interior.

Flower Shop, Oxo Tower, South Bank, SE1
Wingate & Moon

This shop is a small but beautifully formed response to a retail classic – the florist – that incorporates a range of eclectic interests on the part of the client. Sited on the bottom floor of the Oxo Tower on the South Bank, this is the second shop that the client had opened, following on from a successful 1997 store in Finsbury Park and an innovative foldaway stall in Paddington station.

The Oxo Tower shop is deliberately dark and cavern-like, allowing flowers to be spotlit and providing a sense of mystery and discovery. The client also wanted an 'Indian atmosphere', so a yellow light is used to suggest the hues of an equatorial country.

The display areas for the flowers run along mosaic walls, which undulate along the sides of the shop. Although the mosaic tiles, chosen specifically for their imperfections, sit on a complex timber substructure, they do not feel insubstantial and they contrast well with recessed black areas. The architect claims that these areas of deep, glossy black were influenced by the work of photographer Robert Mapplethorpe. They recede from the high-contrast foregrounds, comprising the colourful flowers, and from the subtler hues of the mosaic wall.

The shop is also an eminently practical environment, with a riven slate floor that repels the water, and a gutter running down the middle of the shop, meaning that the place is easy to clean and the flowers easy to maintain. The sales area and workshop are clad in mineral-fibre panels, and the display system and counter are in concrete with steel frames and teak surfaces. A smoked glass mirror behind the counter finishes the job and prevents the interior from becoming wholly cave-like. This project, simple as it is, is a gem, showing what can be done with limited space and budget.

Fushi eternal living

Fushi store, Duke of York Square, Chelsea, SW3
Caulder Moore

Successful visual identities are based as much on consistency as on moments of design genius. So often, a decent graphic identity is let down by a poor interior design, or a great building destroyed by terrible signage.

Caulder Moore were commissioned by health food and beauty product retailer Fushi not only to come up with a design for their first stand-alone store (previously the line had been sold at a concession in Selfridges), but also to consider the packaging of the products, a graphic identity and a new website.

The result gives a real coherence to a brand that relies on a certain neutrality – antiseptic or zen-like, depending on how you look at it – for its image. Fushi (Japanese for 'eternal living', apparently) sells organic products ranging from freshly made fruit juices to bathing oils, and has built its business on such twenty-first-century activities as detoxing, relaxing and getting over hangovers.

In line with the new-age brand language ("the aim is to encourage a more balanced inner-self that promotes outer wellbeing through holistic remedies", states the PR material), the interior design of the shop feels like a stab at a futuristic health shop or laboratory – like the milk bars in *A Clockwork Orange*, or the kind of place that might sell canned oxygen in a post-nuclear apocalyptic world.

The use of planes of materials – neutral grey tiles for the floor, white rendered walls, and mirrors and timber for the bars – allows the products to speak for themselves and enhances the apparent transparency of the merchandise. Even the simple text and pictures on the packaging – spare sans-serif fonts and images of clear-skinned young women – seem to speak of an unthreatening and pure product. If you are the kind of person who would buy Fushi, then this interior will provide the ideal environment in which to do it.

Gibo boutique, Conduit Street, W1
Cherie Yeo/Julie Verhoeven

New fashion label Gibo's new shop is a wonderful expression of the values of the label that it houses. Architect Cherie Yeo (an ex-employee of flavour-of-the-month architects David Adjaye and William Russell) and the label's designer, Julie Verhoeven, were friends before the project began, and Yeo's stated aim was to "not steal the limelight. I wanted to design a quiet space so as not to steal the show from the clothes." They came up with a building that has a wealth of design ideas, but enough flexibility to allow for customization.

The site was difficult – just 6 m (20 ft) wide, forcing the 170 sq m (1830 sq ft) of floor area into a long, thin corridor. Yeo's strategy pulls the visitor into the space through a combination of seductive surfaces and tricks of perspective, with the many new interventions reading as pieces of furniture.

This is a project, unlike so many fashion boutique fit-outs, that has an interest in the history and memory of the building. Prior to Gibo acquiring the space, it had been a shop for Alexander McQueen, and before that a bridal shop. When the previous interior was stripped away, Yeo and Verhoeven discovered sketches, mouldings and architraves behind the previous lining, and decided to integrate them into the new interior. The result is a 14 m (45 ft) 'doodle wall' of sketches, builders' scribbles and football-related graffiti, to which Verhoeven plans to invite artists to add.

The rest of the interior allows for constant shifting and changing. One wall, made of Corian, has thousands of tiny drilled holes for pegs to be inserted in a variety of patterns so that clothing can be hung from them. The centrepiece of the shop is the garment rails designed by Yeo that can be folded away into recesses in a concrete wall. These structures can be configured in a variety of different ways and are anchored by holes in the floor.

Customers often ask the shop's employees when the interior is going to be finished. Which is exactly what the architect and client intended.

Griffin boutique and showroom, Portobello Road, W11
El Ultimo Grito/Nathalie de Leval

El Ultimo Grito is a design practice that professes to specialize in industrial and interior design, but is equally known for work that explores the boundaries of design, art and architecture. The studio was established in 1997 by Spanish pair Rosario Hurtado and Roberto Feo, who came up with their ironic epithet – which roughly translates as 'the latest thing'.

They have since worked for such prestigious furniture manufacturers as Moroso and Magis, as well as some blue-chip clients (including Bloomberg), and have designed products such as a new coffee machine for Italian firm Lavazza. The Griffin store is one of their most famous projects – an inexpensive but very successful fit-out for this small but hip fashion label. The exterior is very simple, with a large glass shopfront and neon sign adding a touch of seedy glamour. Inside, the small space is allowed to be as flexible as possible, with the addition of eccentric but functioning elements.

The most obvious of these elements is the field of hooks suspended from the ceiling, allowing for a variety of hanging installations. These include strange coat hangers with extended necks for garments, which can be hung in a huge variety of patterns to help define spatial boundaries. The concept is that the space allows itself to be reinterpreted every season by a designer or artist. El Ultimo Grito's initial fit-out featured tree trunks hanging from the ceiling, with a garden shed in their midst as an office.

Hurtado and Feo's concept drawings consisted simply of a box with hooks on the ceiling, and a comment scrawled underneath: "Nothing, so anything you bring in creates a new shop" – effectively making the entire space into the window display. As a response to a brief from a client with plenty of her own ideas, it is both appropriate and liberatingly simple.

Mandarina Duck boutique, Conduit Street, W1
Marcel Wanders/Harper Mackay

Italian fashion label Mandarina Duck has manoeuvred itself into a position of almost unassailable cool. Its luggage – with which the company started – is the last word in minimalist contemporary, and is standard uniform for a certain type of urban traveller.

One of the main reasons the company has been able to develop such a position is its patronage of good design. Quite apart from its products, it commissioned graphic design legend Peter Saville to design its logo and branding, employed hip Dutch designers NL Architects and Droog to design the Paris boutique, and created an amazing landscape of stacked tables, designed by Angelo Micheli and Studio Lucchi, in Rome.

For its London base (or embassy, as Mandarina Duck calls these flagship stores), the label went to a former member of Dutch product design collective Droog, Marcel Wanders. Wanders's work until then had consisted almost entirely of furniture, so it is no surprise that the main interest in this interior are the placed elements rather than the surfaces of the building itself.

The most obvious of these elements is the array of yellow and silver mannequins, inspired in part by *Gulliver's Travels*, that gather around the feet of the centrepiece – a polyurethane mannequin 7 m (23 ft) tall. These models, which come in both male and female versions, have a unique feature: they breathe. Get close enough, and you can see their chests slowly inflating and deflating. This is copied on a larger scale by the silver tyvek-covered wall that forms the backdrop to the staircase. The whole wall breathes, as a pump behind takes in air through holes in the giant silver pillowy façade, referring obliquely to a range of inflatable handbags designed by Wanders for Mandarina Duck.

The rest of the project, with brown carpets and smoked glass cabinets, is less remarkable, but the mannequins have caused quite a stir. Are they anatomically correct? Are the male figures too Afro-Caribbean? Are the female ones too short and aggressive? Like all of Wanders's work, they certainly provide a talking point.

Michel Guillon Optometrist, Kings Road, SW3
Kitchen Rogers Design/DA Studio

Kitchen Rogers Design is a practice that has designed at a wide variety of scales, from door handles for FSB and seating for Edra to interiors in Paris, London and Kuwait. Their widely published Comme des Garçons boutique in Paris, completed in collaboration with the fashion label's mastermind, Rei Kawakubo, has been the most important example of their approach so far, with its red fibreglass surfaces and red cubes of furniture that move around the room by remote control.

Partner Abe Rogers is the son of legendary high-tech architect Richard Rogers, but it is not so much technology that runs as a theme through Kitchen Rogers's work, but rather kinetic movement and mechanics. Previous examples of the practice's work in this country include an installation in 2001 at Top Shop in the Bluewater shopping centre, where a glowing wall of magenta and cyan displayed Top Shop products slowly but constantly in motion.

Michel Guillon is, at first sight, a beautiful, otherworldly interior that adequately displays its merchandise – spectacles. However, the designers have been able to integrate a kinetic sculpture in the form of the wall running down one side of the showroom. This blue surface is 14 m (46 ft) long, and is punctured by 462 regularly spaced white-walled recesses, each containing a pair of glasses. With the help of motors behind the wall, each pair of glasses can be pushed forward, forming what the designers call a "dynamic landscape", intended to draw passers-by into the store.

The basement area contains the more private consultancy pods, which are also clad in blue and have medically sterile white interiors. The building superbly demonstrates not just the interest of the architects in integrating machines and architecture, but also their sure touch with materials and their sense of glamour and event.

Marni boutique, Sloane Street, SW1
Sybarite

For a practice so clearly influenced by the firm for which the
partners previously worked – Future Systems – Sybarite is forging
quite a name for itself as the darling of the style press. Appearances
in *Vogue*, *Elle Decoration* and *Bazaar* suggest that the undulating
surfaces of its work are appealing to a wider demographic than
most young practices can hope to hit.

Sybarite's work is clearly derived from the blob aesthetic made
famous by Future Systems, architects of previous Marni stores in
New York, Tokyo and Paris, and this Sloane Street shop is strongly
reminiscent of Future Systems's Ferrari motor show stand (2001).
They even hired the same company to construct the Marni
staircase as Future Systems used for their fit-out of New Look on
Oxford Street (see pages 88–89). However, the quality of finish
that has been achieved by such a young practice (the partners
Torquil McIntosh and Simon Mitchell are thirty and thirty-two)
suggests that they could move on to greater things.

The main objective of the design was to link the two levels of
the boutique by stretching a white resin floor from ground to first
floor by way of a specially fabricated staircase that looks as if it has
been cut out of this sheer surface. The design also connects the
stainless steel displays between the different floor areas, turning
them into zoomorphic elements that lead the customer through
the shop.

The red of the ceiling is offset by the white lighting pods
that hover over the space, and the sunken floor areas are also
coloured in vivid fire-engine red. This interior will require
meticulous attention to keep it as pristine as it appears in these
pictures, but it remains a great example of boutique interior
design as bombastic performance.

New Look, Oxford Street, W1
Future Systems

Future Systems has long been one of the great visionaries of the British architectural scene, but its buildings remained largely unbuilt for a good proportion of its history. It has now been able to build at a large scale, and it is in the retail sector that it has found many of the greatest opportunities, including its biggest project to date – the silver disc-clad Selfridges store in Birmingham's Bull Ring shopping centre.

The boutiques that the practice had designed previously were mainly for high-end fashion brands – they developed stores for Marni in London and Milan, and created the famous and hugely successful Comme des Garçons shop in New York. New Look, the budget high-street fashion chain, would seem an unlikely client, but it is a brand that has built its pre-eminent market position on having a keen sense of the warp and weft of style and design.

Future Systems were employed, said one New Look director, to make a "fantastic entrance to hoover people off the street". They have certainly done that. Behind the yellow glass doors lies a spectacular polished stainless steel staircase, clearly visible from the street.

This leads up to a more upmarket section, with slightly more expensive merchandise. The space is unified by a glowing caterpillar-like installation that winds through the aisles. In other areas, the concrete of the building is left exposed and augmented with innovative ways of displaying the merchandise, such as cantilevered Perspex trays containing shoes and lingerie hung from green mattresses. The glittering surface underfoot contrasts with the raw wall finishes and is made from glass balls set in white resin.

The Future Systems pieces in the shop look almost retro-fitted in places, and this may be because they have been designed to be replicated in many of the other 500 New Look stores in the country. They will provide a welcome touch of camp glamour for many a dowdy high street.

Oki-Ni boutique, Savile Row, W1
6a Architects

The brief for this fashion retailer's largest shop was one of the most difficult an architect could face. Oki-Ni – which means 'thank you' in Osakan dialect – is a retailer that sells exclusively customized pieces of clothing from such design houses as Evisu, Levi's and Adidas. Although it has premises, these are just to allow customers to try on clothes before they order them online. The architects 6a were given the job after a small competition – the three-partner practice had built nothing together before this, and the boutique went on to become a multi-award-winning calling card for the young firm.

They came up with a concept that is intended to be "a comfortable social setting in which to appreciate clothes". To this end, the architects decided that the setting for the garments should be a large oak 'tray' defining the space, with clothes haphazardly hung over the timber walls and arranged on piles of felt mats, which perform as adaptable pieces of furniture and display surfaces. The oak tray is slightly fan-shaped, which gives it the feel of a stage. This theatricality is noticeable more from the street than from inside, and is a subtle counterpoint to the deliberately relaxed feel of the interior.

Lighting is from a field of standard fluorescents, creating another layer in the design. There are very few details here, giving the space a certain coolness and allowing the clothes to become the focus of the customers' attention. Concealed behind the freestanding timber walls are services, changing rooms and access to the shop's office.

This brilliantly simple solution has been repeated at different scales in other locations: there are now Oki-Ni concessions within stores all over Japan and in other UK cities, all of which use the idea of freestanding walls and piles of felt as display backgrounds.

Patrick Cox at Charles Jourdan, New Bond Street, W1
Brinkworth

One of the pleasures of interior design for the commercial world is that the process of design and construction is very short compared with that of building something from the ground up. Boutique interiors have a short shelf-life – two years is often the maximum amount of time a high-end fashion house would leave an interior before refitting it.

An extreme version of this is Adam Brinkworth's creation for the launch of Patrick Cox's latest collection of shoes and bags at the Charles Jourdan shop in New Bond Street. The installation was only in place for two days, and it embodies the gloriously profligate attitude to showmanship that runs through the core of the fashion industry.

Brinkworth transformed the existing space with the help of velvet drapes concealing a stage set of real drama. The shop window was hung with red velvet and lit as an opulent signboard to the street. Inside the red velvet gave way to black drapes running floor to ceiling along both walls, with red lights in the floor.

The centrepiece of the interior, though, was the bonded glass lightbox running the entire length of the room like a catwalk, and on which the shoes were displayed, lit from below and by spotlights in the ceiling. The effect of the heavy, dark drapes and the central luminescent box was dramatic. Above the lightbox ran a matching gloss-black ceiling panel, its highly polished surface reflecting images of the shoes, the dancers and the visitors.

Continuing the bordello aesthetic, visitors could also please themselves by watching the silhouettes of three dancers gyrating behind a backlit projection screen. This was interior design as event, and its ephemerality made it all the more special – the quintessential interior-designed fashion statement.

Peter Jones, Sloane Square, SW3
John McAslan + Partners

Retail buildings in major cities have often taken on iconic status, becoming indelibly associated with the identity of their respective cultures. One thinks of the gallerias of Milan, Galeries Lafayette in Paris, Bloomingdale's in New York, KaDeWe in Berlin, or Harrods in our own city. However, the Modern Movement in the UK produced depressingly few retail buildings of note. Perhaps the only one is Peter Jones in Chelsea, designed by William Crabtree in the 1930s. It is Britain's most highly listed department store, at Grade 2*.

However, the store had long since lost its lustre as a shopping destination in comparison with the contemporary boutiques of the nearby King's Road or the modern interiors of Selfridges and Harvey Nichols. Its interior was incoherent and depressingly institutional, belying the drama of its iconic exterior. John McAslan + Partners were employed to resolve the warren-like circulation and dingy shopping floors. Although major architectural moves were limited due to the listing, they have impressively returned a sense of grandeur and coherence to the store.

The refurbishment's first phase was completed in 2002, the major task of which was to extend an existing light-well up through the full height of the building and to insert zigzagging escalators to improve the circulation and provide a major orientation point on every floor of the store.

The original building had provided generous facilities for staff, including roof-top squash courts and a ballroom that had been appropriated as storage space. These have been reclaimed as a new restaurant. Much of the money spent on the project (£100,000,000 in total) is invisible, used to replace out-of-date servicing and operational facilities, but the refurbishment does manage to balance the social aspirations of this much-loved Modernist classic with the contemporary needs of an international department store.

Stella McCartney boutique, Old Bond Street, W1
Universal Design Studio

Universal's interior for Stella McCartney's first London store demonstrates two significant and seemingly contradictory trends in commercial interior design – the impulse to provide a vision of a global brand consistent throughout many premises around the world, and the desire to give the consumer a sense of discovery and individuality in a retail environment.

Universal Design Studio had already completed McCartney's flagship store in New York when they got the job of converting an old art gallery in a Georgian townhouse on Old Bond Street into over 1000 sq m (11,000 sq ft) of headquarters and shop. The New York store used some strongly geometric patterns and rich hangings along with an eccentric selection of custom-made furniture, and this approach was replicated in London with very different results.

Key elements from the original building, such as skylights and arches, were reworked, and some original mouldings and picture rails have been restored. In the retail space, natural imagery dominates (branches and trees painted on the floor and walls), but the cabinets and clothes rails are in minimally detailed structural glass, which is coloured a wonderfully camp pink.

Achieving consistency with the New York store is done reasonably subtly – bespoke tiles designed originally for New York are used again as a backdrop along one wall. However, the store retains a feel of individuality, with a fairy-tale mural, designed by McCartney herself, filling another wall. Other materials include limestone, polished black granite and smoked oak floors.

The interior reflects the fashion designer's interest in an eclecticism that is unafraid of using found objects, materials or patterns. Handmade wallpaper and hand-printed fabrics suggest old school luxury, and the overall impression is consistent with McCartney's sensual, romantic and somewhat nostalgic clothes.

Boutique concession, Topshop, Oxford Street, W1
Tank

With the likes of New Look, Miss Selfridge and Hennes & Mauritz in hot pursuit, high-street budget clothes retailer Topshop has had to keep on its toes to remain the favourite shopping destination of teenage girls and poverty-stricken shoppers who want a bit of ersatz designer wear.

One arm of its strategy is its new Boutique line, a designer range by up-and-coming designers at bargain prices. The setting for this new range at the flagship Topshop store near Oxford Circus has been designed to set itself apart from the glorified jumble sale that forms the normal retail environment in this titanic store.

Super-cool design collective Tank were employed to design a discrete part of the Oxford Street store to accommodate the range, and also to come up with a graphic identity and packaging for the Boutique concept. Tank, which grew out of the team that founded the fashion magazine of the same name, intended to create a place that was a respite from the rest of the shop.

The area is wrapped in a sloping ribbon of black Perspex, inspired by the black strips used to censor letters in wartime. This, along with the monolithic white Corian cabinets, clear acrylic shelves and white resin floor inside, is intended to suggest erasure of, or interference with, the bazaar-like atmosphere of the rest of the store. Architect Shumon Basar says: "The challenge was to create something new and different in one of the most saturated retail environments in London. There's no way we could be louder than Topshop, so our strategy was to create something like white noise to cancel that out."

The ribbon perimeter selectively conceals and reveals the environment within and the clothes on display. It is not about calmness, but about a brand of cool that lends an edgy exclusivity.

Whistles retail concept, Islington, N1
Brinkworth

Brinkworth is an interior design practice that is able to combine convincing space-making strategy and a taste for glamorous materials with a knowledge of branding and how to create successful corporate environments.

Brinkworth's store for fashion retailer Whistles in Islington is intended to be the blueprint for a series of shops to be rolled out in Brighton, Bluewater shopping centre, Wimbledon, Glasgow, Leeds and Guildford, and extended to a concession in Harrods. The brief was to create an environment sympathetic to the clothes, but also appealing to the Whistles target customer, whom they characterize as "feminine, intelligent, humorous, and quirky with a strong sense of discovery".

The response has been to create a wilfully eclectic interior behind the acid-pink neon lettering that signals the store to the street. The site for the Islington store is a long, thin floorplate with a handsome bay window facing the street. Brinkworth took a bold line, electing to divide the floor area into three zones. Rather than allowing the space to be immediately legible to the consumer, the rear third of the shop is concealed behind a mirrored promontory, playing on the client's desire to allow customers a sense of discovery as they look around the store.

The immediate scene on entering the shop is both striking and rather unsettling. A forest of mannequins is mounted on oak plinths of different heights, showing off the clothes, but also dwarfing the visitor among the impassive, decapitated figures. The second zone is an interstitial one between this initial mannequin-world and the semi-hidden room at the back. The division works wonderfully, giving a corridor-like space the proportions of a series of rooms.

Materially, the project sparkles – a combination of antique finishes, such as high-gloss aubergine lacquer, stained oak flooring and wallpaper, with such contemporary tricks as a huge light-box extending the length of one wall and inscribed with the same pattern as the wallpaper.

The store is on a thoroughfare swiftly descending into an area of chain restaurants and high-street multiples, where it appears as a rose among thorns. One hopes this identity will not become watered down as it is reproduced for other stores.

Exercising and grooming

Daniel Galvin hair salon, George Street, W1
Caulder Moore Architects

When we go for a haircut, we expect more than just a short back and sides or a shampoo and set. Today's service industries are in the business of selling an experience that will involve the customer fully. We want our hairdressers to serve perfect coffee, and we want the interiors to be as much a statement about us as the haircuts they're selling.

It comes as no surprise, then, that a West End hair salon should have wanted the atmosphere not of a barber shop, but of a boutique hotel: it treats its customers to lounge areas, a coffee bar and individual styling stations that are bespoke. Not for Daniel Galvin (known in the trade as the 'king of colour') the traditional lines of barbers' chairs facing mirrors.

The salon interior is an object lesson in branding, but, perhaps for that very reason, feels less than intimate. The aesthetic is generic contemporary, although lavishly realized, and there is little internal coherence. The reflective polished stone floors and the long, low, minimal bench under the staircase are straight out of John Pawson's work. The 'feature' staircase uses glass and steel to bring what one presumes is seen as a more contemporary note. It is hardly Eva Jiricna, however.

The environment provides the comforts one would expect: independent temperature control for different areas of the salon, good levels of lighting for work with hair colouring, and a two-storey water feature, all of which contribute to a relaxed atmosphere. This is what Daniel Galvin's customers want. These are people who could as easily get their hair done in the salons of Milan, Paris or New York, and the interior would feel at home in any of these fashion capitals. It is not consciously a London environment, but is operating at the transnational level of a world-leading brand. Although it is proficient, this was never going to be a cutting-edge piece of design. It does, however, demonstrate what clients of this type require for the good of their international profile.

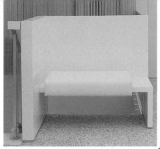

Fordham White hair salon, Soho, W1
Hudson Featherstone Architects

As a practice, Hudson Featherstone (re-formed in August 2002 into two separate practices, Hudson Architects and Featherstone Associates) sometimes felt out of step with prevailing architectural trends. Anthony Hudson and Sarah Featherstone made their name with a series of playful, idiosyncratic projects that rejected the austerity of many of their contemporaries' work without resorting to the over-egged formalism of such maximalists as Will Alsop.

Any practice that could put their name to an exhibition called *Who's Afraid of Visual Candy?* (curated by furniture manufacturer SCP in 2000) was hardly going to rely on unadorned white render interiors. The practice's work always celebrated colour and ornamentation with wit and charisma, and their hair salon for the young hairstylist duo Fordham White is no exception. The frontage for this small salon in the heart of Soho was only 3 m (10 ft) wide, so it required both a light touch with the interior fittings and a big effort to provide a striking street frontage.

The front part of the salon was conceived as a deliberately ambiguous space emphasizing relaxation and indulgence, featuring a custom-designed, rococo-esque seat as a centrepiece, covered in an opulent Marie Antoinette fabric. The long south wall is a simple pink surface, with nooks cut out of it to accommodate a television and to display products. This is tempered by more contextual references in the shopfront itself: a large rose-tinted plate-glass expanse, referencing the sex shops of the area. The façade also has a large section of mirrored wall punched through it, giving passing clients a before-and-after view of their haircuts. This is a satisfying solution to the architects' stated aim of providing a striking and distinctive frontage without resorting to conventional hanging signs.

The sex-shop references continue inside, with the 'hairy' ceiling covered in translucent tassels – an echo of the tassels across doorways in the seedier establishments of Soho. These tassels are taken further at the back of the shop, where they form a floor-to-ceiling forest, creating a sensuous environment for a health-and-beauty spa.

The space widens towards the back, and it is here that the business of washing and cutting hair takes place, with ten stylists' chairs all encircled by rose walls and bronze-tinted mirrors. Every surface has something of the kitsch world of the Soho madame about it.

There is something thrilling about the boldness of this interior, and Sarah Featherstone and Anthony Hudson are architects who are not afraid to see interior design as an exercise in creating a commercially viable, opulent, ironic and jokey environment. While interiors in Soho seem to veer more and more towards minimalist noodle bars and exposed-concrete drinking dens, Fordham White

hair salon is a joy, packing humour and charm into a tiny envelope and a budget of just £270,000. With Featherstone and Hudson having gone their separate ways, one hopes that this will double their subversive influence on architecture and design, which has a tendency to take itself too seriously.

KXGYMUK, Brompton Cross, SW3
Thorp Design

This area of London is filled with conspicuously consuming types with no shortage of income just waiting to be disposed on the latest bit of rich-chic. KXGYMUK, pronounced 'kicks', is a boutique sports club aimed squarely at this demographic. It is possibly the most lavishly appointed gym in London, fitted out with a less-than-understated opulence. Thorp Design has completed house, yacht and plane interiors for many extremely rich clients, and this job was designed to justify the £2000 per year (plus £1000 joining fee) that KXGYMUK punters stump up.

The space occupies the ground floor of the old Harrods depository and used to be a restaurant. The new fit-out hides the exercise rooms at the back of the plan (for privacy) and gives the Draycott Avenue façade a café that appears more like an upmarket restaurant or private members' club.

A small but opulent material palette sets the tone. Wall coverings and doors are of Makasar ebony, with teak furniture throughout. Even the sinks in the changing rooms are Corian units by Italian manufacturer Boffi, and hand-woven carpets stop just short of the walls to reveal diagonally laid teak floors. This is more boutique hotel than local leisure centre.

To create the desired effect, the designer found moments where only bespoke design would do. In the changing rooms, standard non-slip coverings were rejected, and instead individual pieces of limestone were drilled with hundreds of tiny holes and rubber nodules inserted. Also, standard lockers and shelving were rejected in favour of custom-designed teak keyless lockers, with special compartments for valuables and breakables.

Spatially, the building is intended to give its members complete privacy, with individual exercising rooms fitted with top-of-the-range audio-visual equipment as well as exercise machines that can be networked to the internet, enabling members to access their personal trainers anywhere in the world.

It is, in many ways, the complete club environment. Members do not need cash, paying for everything with Bill Amberg-designed key fobs embedded with microchips containing members' bank details. The owner claims his intention was to make "a club that just happens to be a gym". The richness of the fit-out supports this intention without making anything too aesthetically challenging.

Metis Physiotherapy, Drury Lane, WC2
Detail

A restaurateur and a physiotherapist may seem an unlikely team, but it is a combination that spawned the first boutique physiotherapy clinic in London, in the spectacular setting of the old Theatre Royal on Drury Lane.

Restaurateur Ronnie Truss (the man behind the modish Bank and Fish!) teamed up with sports physiotherapist David West to create Metis, a new physiotherapy practice catering to the stars of sport and dance. The designer, Gordon Russell of Detail architects and designers, got the job after working on a number of projects for Truss. According to Russell, "Ronnie used David's practice and recognized that although physiotherapists were professional, they don't do it in a professional environment. There was nowhere to get this treatment in comfort and style."

Truss and Russell decided on the remarkable site together, managing to lease an old scenery painting warehouse, known as The Long Dock, within the Grade 1 listed Theatre Royal on Drury Lane. The main fabric of the Theatre Royal dates from 1812 (although parts of the building are attributed to Christopher Wren), and permanent alterations were strictly outlawed due to heritage interests. This particular space had been used as a junk room since the 1970s.

The project thus became a series of five prefabricated, mirror-clad pods irregularly spaced on the ground floor and the installation of a new, freestanding mezzanine floor, which hangs from new exposed steel beams. The open plan accommodates office space and break-out areas for staff. The pods themselves are colour-coded and house the treatment rooms. These rooms are without windows but are decorated with floor-to-ceiling murals of theatre interiors.

According to Russell, "We spent a lot of time persuading interested parties that we could alter the existing fabric without making irreversible changes. We really didn't want to do much to the building anyway. Our brief was to make it very practical, but express the fact that these guys are at the cutting edge of what they do. So we just dropped these pods out of the sky that don't touch the walls."

Spa at the Mandarin Oriental Hotel, Knightsbridge, SW1
Eric Parry Architects

There is a fine tradition of building spa and bath houses in Europe, particularly in the old Alpine spa towns. Peter Zumthor's bath house at Vals in Switzerland, with its almost religious treatment of the rituals of bathing and cleansing, has become one of the quintessential icons of contemporary architecture. Eric Parry's spa at the five-star Mandarin Oriental derives much more from this lineage than from any notion of a spa that might have been developed in this country. The emphasis here is on the relaxed and serious application of alternative treatments and relaxation techniques in an environment that is strongly hermetic and cocoon-like.

Situated in the basement of the hotel, the spa is arranged around a central corridor embellished with pieces of art commissioned by the architect that look like decorations from an ancient Mayan tomb, expressed in rich timber and dark grey Zimbabwean granite.

The reception area leads to a monolithic masonry staircase with bronze handrails that accesses the lower level. Top-lit curtains hide the view of the other corridors. The calmness of this area prepares the visitor for the rituals below. The first stage involves a sanarium, steam room, vitality pool with mineral water, and hydrotherapy body jets. This is just preparation for one of the wide range of therapies available in the eight individual treatment rooms. These rooms are lavishly appointed, with a high level of textured surfaces such as horse hair for doors and partitions and an off-white craquelé lacquer inside.

Perhaps the most spectacular space is the stone-lined pool, which is separated from the steam room by a simple veil of etched glass. This is a somehow timeless, therapeutic space, in which luxurious relaxation seems a natural result. Materially and spatially, the design works at a range of scales, emphasizing the individual and demanding a pleasing slowness in the consumption of its facilities.

Exhibiting and performing

Almeida Theatre, Islington, N1
Burrell Foley Fisher

The Almeida has written itself into theatrical history since its
foundation in 1978, with previous directors Ian MacDiarmid and
Jonathan Kent making it one of the most artistically vibrant
theatres in the capital. In addition, MacDiarmid and Kent initiated
the refurbishment project that led to the theatre taking its current
form, designed by Burrell Foley Fischer.

The building, which was built in the late nineteenth century
by Robert Roumieu, an architect of Huguenot extraction, had been
famous for being draughty and letting in the rain – as well as for
hosting moments of great theatre. In 1999 a lottery grant was
secured for the refit, and the Almeida decamped for temporary
stays first at the Gainsborough Studios in Shoreditch, and then at
a bus garage in King's Cross for two years.

Meanwhile, Burrell Foley Fischer faced the dilemma of a
much-loved and characterful space that was unsuited to the
demands of modern drama. The architect elected, sensibly, to try
to retain as far as possible the sense of a found space that existed
in the auditorium, and augmented the front-of-house facilities
with a distinctively contemporary low-rise extension next door.

The auditorium remains pretty basic, with no wings and no
barriers between public and performers. However, the seats are
considerably more comfortable, and the leak-free roof has been
made higher to accommodate larger-scale lighting and acoustic
equipment and air-conditioning. Backstage, the architect has
been able to carve out a wealth of new spaces, including a props
room, costume store and workshop, as well as rebuilding the
dressing-rooms.

If the new additions are a little soulless, this is more than
compensated by the skill with which the architect has retained the
atmosphere of the original Almeida. It has lost none of its magic,
and MacDiarmid and Kent have left a fitting legacy to new director
Michael Attenborough.

Concert hall refurbishment, Barbican Centre, EC1
Caruso St John

Caruso St John would certainly balk at being described as interior designers. The practice, headed by Peter St John and Adam Caruso, is one of the most serious and exciting in the country, having shot to prominence after the completion of the highly acclaimed New Art Gallery Walsall. Since then, the practice has found it difficult to find work of any size in the UK, but is one of the architects involved in the refurbishment of Chamberlin Powell & Bon's iconic Barbican Centre.

Although the main refurbishment is being carried out by Allford Hall Monaghan Morris, Caruso St John was given the £6,000,000 job of refurbishing the concert hall, and creating a new ceiling to help the acoustics in the auditorium.

The acoustic strategy, formulated in collaboration with noted Chicago-based acousticians Kirkegaard Associates, was aimed at making the Barbican the pre-eminent concert hall in Britain. In Caruso St John the Barbican found architects with a real enthusiasm for the existing building, who elected to retain the acoustically troublesome wooden inner lining of the hall. This meant that the building was not much changed visibly, apart from the spectacular new canopy and ceiling.

The canopy is made of twenty-five suspended acoustic reflectors coated in Rimex, an acid-etched stainless steel notably used by Frank Gehry on the exterior of his Experience Music Project in Seattle. This treatment of the steel means that the material has a naturally varied red sheen, and the whole canopy changes colour depending on where you sit and what light is shining on it. The subtly varied angles of the reflectors also give the ceiling a fabric-like texture, and this vermilion surface forms a wonderful counterpoint to the heather, moss and peat colours of the seats below.

The suspended panels conceal a wealth of servicing, access gantries, lighting rigs and ductwork, and the canopy over the stage can be adjusted to reveal lighting rigs and speaker clusters, needed for the hall's other life as a conference venue. Despite this concealment, new uplighters do reveal the concrete coffers of the original ceiling, showing the old through the cracks in the new.

Caruso St John describes the ceiling as "a beautiful chandelier", and it genuinely adds to the grandeur of attending a concert at the Barbican. However, the scheme is also supremely functional and, although improving acoustic performance is far from an exact science, the ceiling has improved such matters in the hall considerably. The mid-range is reportedly much clearer, and penetration to the back of the hall has been enhanced.

The appointment of Caruso St John for one of the most prominent cultural institutions in the capital could prove a brave and forward-looking step, signalling a move away from the grand old men of British high-tech – Norman Foster, Richard Rogers *et al.* – towards a more civic, sensuous and material architecture. The meticulous realization of the Barbican hall should help British architecture and design move forward to rediscover a link to the classics of high Modernism, such as the Barbican Centre itself.

Camden Arts Centre, NW1
Tony Fretton Architects

Camden Arts Centre was originally launched in 1965 to provide the local community with classes in the arts, and it has retained this mission while developing into an important venue for world-class contemporary art. The building it occupies, however, has always been a characterful yet problematic home for the organization. Set in a library built in 1897, it was entered through a grand portico reached by a stone stairway from ground level. As well as causing problems for disabled visitors to the centre, the entrance meant that the basement was a neglected resource, with a series of offices and studios of variable quality. Tony Fretton's scheme reconfigures the basement as the main access to the centre, creating a new glazed front entrance at this lower level that leads through to the new and generous reception and bookshop area. At the back of this route is the new garden room housing a café and looking out onto a terrace in the garden, which has been landscaped by art/architecture collective Muf.

The treatment of the interior was contingent upon and defined largely by the small budget. Walls are painted white and rooms have been cleaned up, with new roof-lights and air-conditioning installed. New interventions are subtle, but on closer inspection reveal themselves as charming, if slightly eccentric in places. The project does not attempt to dramatize the difference between the new and old building fabric, but instead creates moments of ambiguity, such as the red terrazzo floors in the new reception area and staircase that could be mistaken for an original finish. The ironmongery also has this strange ambiguity, with customized Bauhaus door handles in gold finishes creating a slightly disorienting sense of history (they are not quite contemporary, nor are they naturally part of this nineteenth-century building).

Art centres such as Camden get much of their charm from the sense of their being well-used and customized over time. Fretton has managed to retain this attraction by avoiding antiseptic contemporary aesthetics in favour of a richer, more idiosyncratic look.

Coronet Cinema,
Elephant and Castle, SE1
Kracka

The site of the Coronet Cinema has been used as a place of
entertainment since the seventeenth century. Its heyday as the
Elephant and Castle Theatre in the late nineteenth century saw it
play host to, among others, the child star Charlie Chaplin. In 1928
the theatre was remodelled as a spectacular thousand-seater Art
Deco cinema, before being modernized in 1966. It subsequently
fell into disrepair and was bought in 2001 by the Pure Group, an
entertainment business that had already made a huge success of
Heaven nightclub in Covent Garden.

The plan was to turn the dclapidated cinema into a club and
concert venue at the same time retaining its function as a
cinema. The building, something of a forgotten gem, wasn't listed,
which gave design consultant Kracka free rein with the interior.
However, the £2,000,000 budget would not have allowed for a
complete refit of the space, and the practice decided to retain and
restore many period features while stripping out the additions
made in the 1960s and adding several identifiably contemporary
interventions.

The journey through the building begins in the foyer, decked
out in purple rubber tiles, then passes through a corridor lit from
above by an elaborate light sculpture. All this, though, pales in
comparison with the enormous ground-floor space, with its 17 m
(56 ft) ceiling replete with Art Deco details, and the original
proscenium-arch stage on which a cinema-quality screen can be
erected when the Coronet is in use as a cinema.

The new bar on the ground floor is in a generic industrial mode,
but the decadence levels rise on the upper floors, which feature
tacky but fun leather seating decorated with gold leaf.

The 'superclub' phenomenon that swept Britain in the 1990s did
not produce many genuinely distinguished physical environments,
but the Coronet seems to be part of a new generation of these
places, in which more emphasis is put on design. Whether the
punters care about this very much is moot, but it helps the Coronet
to be much more than just a barn for dancing in.

Electric Cinema, Portobello Road, W11
Gebler Tooth/Michaelis Boyd Associates

The Electric Cinema has had a long and chequered history. Built in 1910, during cinema's first big surge of popularity, it has since found itself superseded by more modern and accessible premises. Against the odds, though, the cinema survived, albeit in a delapidated state and despite various closures. The Royal Borough of Kensington and Chelsea had taken a pragmatic view and supported a scheme by architecture practice Gebler Tooth to restore and extend the cinema. In the late 1990s Peter Simon, founder of the Monsoon fashion chain, saw the scheme's potential and took it on, and entrepreneur Nick Jones, owner of the Soho House club, bought the lease with a view to making the building a cinema, private members' club and brasserie – a holistic leisure concept designed to make the Electric economically viable.

Gebler Tooth thus began one of the most loving and meticulous restorations of a historic building in recent years. The structure was badly water-damaged, and original colour schemes were a mystery. Through research and years of work, the cinema reopened in 2001 with historic fabric repaired with expressly contemporary additions.

The building is Grade 2* listed, and some innovation was needed to bring the building up to date. The mosaic tile – which had run throughout the original building – was restored, but the rotten timber floor was replaced by concrete with integrated air-conditioning. The old proscenium, its proportions protected by heritage laws, could not be touched, so the architect came up with a new hydraulic screen, which projects outwards when the film starts and extends to widescreen proportions. Accommodation for the 100 spectators in the auditorium is luxurious, with 2.5 m (8 ft) of space between each seat and the one in front, and tables with integrated wine coolers.

Michaelis Boyd and designer Ilse Crawford joined the team to work on the brasserie and members' club areas. The brasserie is inspired by New York restaurants such as Paslis and Balthazar, with a pewter-topped bar and rows of bottles visible behind it. The members' club continues the New York theme, with classic post-war furniture, timber floors and a chainmail curtain giving privacy from the street.

The Hothouse, Hackney, E8
Ash Sakula Architects

The Hothouse is a grass-roots example of the way culture can help transform urban neighbourhoods. Although cultural regeneration has become a watchword for those involved in city regeneration, it usually involves building major new arts institutions that can attract visitors to a previously neglected area, such as Tate Modern in Southwark. The Hothouse is intended as a much more community-based project, which brings together local creative industries and artists. It also provides a home for arts group Freeform alongside an events and exhibition space, IT training and design studios.

Architect Ash Sakula has managed to provide all this on an unpromisingly long and narrow site by squeezing a new building next to a railway viaduct and occupying a number of railway arches near London Fields station. The arches have been reconditioned and made into a series of artists' studios. The Hothouse takes its name from the eighteenth-century Loddiges nurseries, which stood near this site and claimed to have "the largest hothouses in the world".

In 2003, the building won an Art for Architecture award from the Royal Society of Arts for a project by artist Maggie Ellenby in collaboration with Ash Sakula. The project consisted of a series of text-based works that engaged with the railway viaduct that runs above the Hothouse. The project's final installation saw words mounted on the roof of the Hothouse, exhorting the viewer to "Breathe in" and "Breathe out". The letters were mounted on slim metal rods, which allowed the letters to rock and sway according to the downdraughts of passing trains.

The building opened in 2003, and future phases hope to provide more floors for Freeform and more studio space. It is a fine example of creative occupation of existing infrastructure and plays an important part in Hackney's embryonic creative quarter, alongside much higher-profile buildings such as the Ocean Music Centre, Hackney Empire and the new Technology and Learning Centre near Hackney Town Hall.

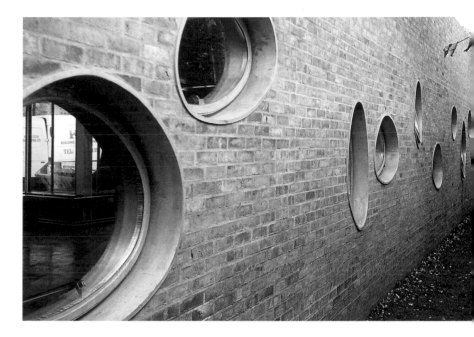

Bethnal Green Museum of Childhood, Bethnal Green, E2
Caruso St John Architects

The Museum of Childhood is a hybrid of a building. The structure was first erected in the 1850s at the Victoria and Albert Museum's South Kensington site to provide temporary accommodation for the collections while the Victoria and Albert's permanent home was being built. In 1872 it was moved to Bethnal Green and reclad to a design by J.W. Wild and Henry Scott. From then on, a changing display of items from the Victoria and Albert Museum's collections was shown here until the early 1970s, when the focus switched entirely to the theme of childhood.

Caruso St John were given the job of refurbishing the building and reorganizing the exhibition, within an extremely small budget, in advance of a planned extension that is awaiting funding. A significant part of the work has been to strip the building of thirty years of additions and to make the dramatic, large-span space legible once again. The ground floor has been completely replanned, with the previous clutter removed and new chocolate-brown furniture functioning as a bookshop, reception desk and café. This allows the ground floor to become an orientating courtyard and reveals its beautiful original mosaic floor.

On the upper floors, the original timber floors have been exposed, and new and reclaimed display cabinets are arranged in compact and dense patterns. The idea has been to create an almost urban arrangement in these upper galleries, a strategy emphasized by the signage, which mimics road signs.

The perspective of this huge space has been emphasized by painting the interior in subtly graded colours, from light to dark pink. The colours were chosen in collaboration with the artist Simon Moretti, who worked on the refurbishment from the beginning of the design stage.

The project will reach its fruition when the new entrance block is built, but this intermediate stage is an important statement of the museum's ambitions.

Museum in Docklands, West India Quay, E14
Purcell Miller Tritton

The received wisdom about museum design is twice bucked over by Purcell Miller Tritton's Museum in Docklands project. For one, it decided that occupying a historical building – a Grade 1 listed warehouse in Docklands dating from 1802 – did not mean that you had to make ruthlessly contemporary additions, marking their difference from the old structure. Purcell Miller Tritton also decided that, rather than making an exhibition space that formed a neutral backdrop to the exhibits, the building itself would be conceived as the primary artefact on display.

The museum tells the history of Docklands, from the Romans to the Reichmanns, with a focus on the nineteenth century, during which it became a hub for global trade and an emblem of European economic power. The building in which the museum sits is a monument to Georgian construction and was in remarkably good condition when the architect came to it. Huge pitch-pine members from the West Indies were affected by dry rot but effectively sound, despite the fact that the building had been derelict since the 1960s.

Purcell Miller Tritton, known for their work in the conservation of historic buildings, decided to make a series of almost invisible repairs and interventions. Timber floors were sanded and repaired in places, and the four new staircases blend with the original masonry. More obvious interventions include the lift shafts, clad in white-painted timber to make a clear division from the historic fabric.

Apart from this, the architect was keen that the space should be allowed to express its scale and history. Floorplates are largely uninterrupted, giving a sense of the depth of plan required by these warehouses. The exhibition design, devised by Haley Sharpe Associates, is also sensitive to the structure, using a system of strapping to affix itself to the building's original fabric.

Museum of London, London Wall, EC1
Wilkinson Eyre

The Museum of London has been one of London's most physically isolated cultural institutions ever since it was built. The building was designed by legendary Festival of Britain architects Powell & Moya and is situated in the heart of the City. However, the building is on a traffic island, isolated from the medieval grain of the City of London and only accessible from Barbican-style walkways. Also, the collection was effectively hidden within a complex circulation arrangement and obscured by the increasingly dowdy-looking interior. The new design provides a new glazed link and entrance lobby and rationalizes the visitors' route through the museum, assisting the museum's curatorial policy of chronological display.

The major new space was opened up by using the void between the museum and the access road below, providing new interpretation facilities and public access to aspects of the museum's conservation work. In all, there is a 70% increase in exhibition space, and infinitely improved access. The building is now much better lit, with natural light pouring from above a new stair into the previously dingy lower levels.

The problem, as with so much architecture that emanates from the British hi-tech tradition, is that the result has more of a feel of a corporate office building than of a cultural institution. The glass balustrades with brushed steel trim and the highly glazed entrance all relate more to the recent history of office design. There are some attempts to reference the toughness of the original Modernist fabric – black Burlington slate is used for some external cladding in a nod to the uncompromising engineering brick of the rotunda building – but in all it feels a little too 'corporate polite' rather than 'Modernist municipal'. Although the project links two Modernist classics – the Barbican and the museum – it doesn't quite match up to either.

The Saatchi Gallery, County Hall, SE1
RHWL

When Charles Saatchi – advertising mogul and svengali of the British art scene – decided to move his gallery from an extremely beautiful contemporary space in St John's Wood to the tacky Edwardiana of County Hall, there were plenty of raised eyebrows.

County Hall has had a curious set of tenants since the Greater London Council was forcibly abolished in 1986. Its Japanese developer-owner has presided over the redevelopment of the heavily listed 1911 building as a 'leisure and cultural centre' to include, among other things, a computer games arcade, a Travel Inn hotel and the FA Premier League Hall of Fame. Into this inauspicious context, Saatchi has inserted two floors of the best of the petulant, modish and compelling work of Hirst, Emin, the Chapmans and the rest of the Britart crew.

The floors that Saatchi decided to occupy are some of the best preserved of the Edwardian building, replete with timber panelling, elaborate inlaid ceilings and vast expanses of parquet flooring. This is no white box gallery.

RHWL, a large commercial architecture practice, was employed to restore the interiors and to make them appropriate for accommodating art. One of the main challenges for the architects was how to configure the warren-like building to accept large-scale artworks. The design does this by allowing certain pieces of the interior to be removed – for example, the bridge that connects the former conference hall to the lobby – to allow for the transportation of works around the building. This is also done on a smaller scale, where oak pediments around the doors of the first-floor rooms can also be removed.

Inside, the Saatchi Gallery provides one of the strangest gallery experiences in London. However, the robust Edwardian interior, designed by Ralph Knott, stands up well to the collection of dissected animal corpses, pools of oil and piles of cigarette butts it now contains. Saatchi has future plans to occupy further floors, and there is talk of him rescuing the disused council chamber at the heart of the building.

The Centenary Galleries, Tate Britain, Millbank, SW1
John Miller & Partners

It must have been tough for Tate Britain when the arriviste Tate Modern opened to such universal acclaim and popularity. The original Tate, in its purpose-built but much-extended home designed by Sidney E.J. Smith in 1897, still had, arguably, the better collection and the more enjoyable environment for looking at art, but lacked the PR power of the new gallery.

It needed its own relaunch, and got it in 2001 when John Miller & Partners completed its new west entrance and the Centenary Galleries. The practice had previously reworked the Whitechapel Gallery for Tate chief Nicholas Serota, and he now brought them in to head the £19,000,000 lottery-funded project. This involved the demolition of four existing galleries, the refurbishing of five further galleries, and the construction of four new ones.

The low-key design of this new interior space is in stark contrast to the international superstar architecture of Tate Modern, and achieves the admirable goal of making the galleries more accessible and adding ample public space to a building that has long lacked coherence. This is mainly done through the generous new reception and orientation area that awaits the visitor just inside the new Manton entrance in the east façade. From this low and pleasingly dark area you can go right to the new bookshop and to the existing café and restaurant, or left to the new galleries.

Some critics have written that the new galleries are almost indistinguishable from the existing building – and opinions are divided over whether this is a good thing or not. Some feel that an opportunity to create a new direction for the Tate Britain galleries has been lost. However, the new staircase circulation area, immaculately detailed in rich limestone, is a huge gain. And the orientation of the grand portico towards the river, with the mean reception area beyond, always felt inadequate when most people approached from the tube station to the north-west. This has now been rectified, and is one the better examples of the easy-access architecture that came out of the National Lottery.

Timothy Taylor Gallery, Dering Street, W1
Eric Parry Architects

The world of the commercial gallery is predicated mainly on chic but neutral white wall space, intended to recede into the background rather than overpower the art. While the rise of rawer, found-space galleries has changed the way we think about displaying artworks, the white box is still, by and large, the choice of most small galleries.

When Timothy Taylor moved his gallery from the Beaux Arts Barn on Bruton Place, he transferred from an old mews building to two floors behind a more conventional shop front on Dering Street. He employed Eric Parry to provide a rich but neutral environment as a background for such artists as Jean-Marc Bustamante, Alex Katz, Richard Patterson and James Rielly, as well as work from the estates of Willem de Kooning, Philip Guston and Tony Smith. The site was a difficult one, with the floorplate an irregular L-shape. Parry put all the office accommodation on the first floor and created a series of ground-floor galleries connected by large openings in white dividing walls.

The key to the project was to connect the two floors and unify the gallery, and this has been achieved with a new precast concrete stair. Upstairs there are showing rooms, offices, a stock room, storage areas, a framing workshop and service rooms. The ground floor has a simple new polished-screed floor, which is conceived partly as a continuation of the pavement outside. Conceptually, the public realm is extended within the building, mediated only by the thin louvred glass of a minimal façade. There is a new shot-peened stainless steel entrance, giving the gallery a contemporary face.

Parry says that the identity of the gallery is defined by its contents rather than by the architecture: "Like switching a light on in a darkened room, the gallery spaces will be given shape and scale by the art that will be placed in them." This illustrates a key aspect of Parry's work, which is very interested in appropriateness, typology and the everyday, rather than the 'event architecture' that characterizes many art spaces.

London Symphony Orchestra/
St Luke's, Old Street, EC1
Levitt Bernstein

Nicholas Hawksmoor would be many people's vote for the greatest British architect of all time. The eighteenth-century genius is known principally for his extraordinary British Baroque churches in east London, the most famous of which, Christ Church, still looms imperiously over Spitalfields Market. St Luke's, consecrated in 1733, became the poor relation of the other churches due to persistent problems with subsidence.

Despite a nineteenth-century renovation, its precarious state culminated in it being declared a dangerous structure in 1959. Its roof was removed, and the shell of the church remained derelict until a lottery grant in 1997 made possible a plan to turn the church into a rehearsal space and education centre for the London Symphony Orchestra.

The existing envelope was saved and restored, but was still not able to support a new roof. Levitt Bernstein, the architects previously responsible for a number of sensitive historical refurbishments (the Royal Exchange Theatre in Manchester) and less sensitive new buildings (the new Stratford Circus theatre), put an entirely new substructure inside the building to take the roof. Tree-like steel columns, as well as acting as supports, conceal a huge amount of servicing and soundproofing. This leaves the interior relatively uninterrupted, yet up to the acoustic and environmental standards required by a world-class orchestra.

A new basement level accommodates a café, a musical instrument store and rooms for the educational part of the building's mission. Digging this basement required the exhumation and reburial of 1000 bodies, and it is now accessed either by two stone staircases, or one spiral one leading down from the new reception.

Although the high-tech visual language of the columns and new roof is not to everyone's taste, the job done by the architects here must rank among their best works, rescuing a building that locals had come to think of as a ruin and bringing another major cultural institution into East London.

The Wapping Project, Wapping, E1
Shed 54

The Wapping Project is one of a growing number of found-space art venues that have been springing up around London in the last decade or so. Tate Modern is the new kid on the block in this context, but the occupation of old industrial buildings began with the private galleries (the original Saatchi gallery, and the Victoria Miro gallery, for example). The Wapping Project has continued this trend.

Jules Wright, dynamic proprietor of the Wapping Project, applied for money from the National Lottery in the mid-1990s but failed to secure a grant to convert the 1890 building. She then set about raising the money herself, from sponsorship and donations, to turn the building into a cavernous arts space and restaurant. The whole thing has something of a Marie Celeste feel to it, with the turbines (which used to pump water around London) still in place next to the chic new restaurant, and the mass of redundant switches and buttons labelled with obsolete instructions and safety advice. Every chipped tile or missing brick is lovingly retained and loaded with history. Wright describes walking into the building for the first time and finding coffee cups still sitting on top of the machines exactly where they had been left when the power station was shut down in 1977.

Shed 54 has added another layer of history to the building, with a series of steel and glass interventions that feel identifiably different from the power station. These do read as a series of interventions rather than a complete rebuilding, despite the work that has been done to restore the Grade 2* listed shell to an inhabitable state.

The materials used by the architect for the new additions are basically steel, slate for floors and the bar surfaces, and glass. The modular steel kitchen is beautifully made, and a great example of the results that are possible when architects work closely with manufacturers.

The single most successful aspect of the scheme is the suspended stairway that leads into the boiler house. It is hung dramatically from the roof by four steel posts, and it is adaptable enough to be transformed for a variety of uses.

Learning

London School of Economics library, Aldwych, WC2
Foster and Partners

Norman Foster is the godfather of the British high-tech architecture scene, but it took some time for him to make his mark on the capital in a big way. Now it seems that every other building completed in London is by Foster, including some of London's most significant landmarks – the Greater London Assembly's Thames-side egg and 30 St Mary Axe (better known as the Gherkin) – and some of its most ordinary office buildings, such as Holborn Circus and Finsbury Square.

The London School of Economics library is a less visible project, but was one of the first of the recent flood to be completed. The LSE is one of Britain's, and Europe's, top academic institutions, with more than 7000 students, and its library is the largest and most important of its type in the world. The university's main buildings are grouped around an atmospheric pedestrian street off the Aldwych and were acquired in stages after the university's institution in 1895.

The four-storey Lionel Robbins building had accommodated the library since 1973 but the structure was in need of expansion and improvement. Foster decided to replace an existing light well with a helical ramp lit from above by a north-facing skylight. This would allow light into the depth of the building and centralize and dramatize circulation around the library.

Materials are not a great concern of Foster's, apart from the use of glass and steel. However, he was forced to learn from severe criticisms of his 1996 library at Oxford University, which was plagued by acoustic problems arising from his use of hard, sound-reflective materials such as glass and natural stone. Here, individual study carrels are situated on the edge of the floor plate, with sound-absorbing book stacks between them and the ramp.

The building is effective and looks good on the university's brochure. It is also a slightly less exuberant version of his spiral ramps for the Reichstag and the Greater London Assembly.

Playgroup at the West London Synagogue, Bayswater, W2
Houlton Taylor Architects

Most ideas of play equipment for nursery-age children would revolve around tubular steel, possibly coated in primary colours, and featuring some strangely malformed animals on springs for the children to ride. Houlton Taylor's nursery for the West London Synagogue comes from a totally different direction, using simple materials and geometrical shapes to provide a landscape on which children can project their own imaginations.

The brief evolved out of conversations with a child education specialist about the various mental associations in terms of form and scale of children at pre-school age. Architect Andrew Houlton says: "I feel that current nurseries with their childish iconography are based on adult impositions of what kids want. Making abstract forms was not an architectural indulgence – we were thinking about the potential of a child's imagination."

Much of the £600,000 budget for the project was spent on refurbishing the existing listed 1920s building. The most visible part of the project is the creation of two pieces of play furniture on the top floor. These divide the room into three, accommodating three different age groups, and are conceived as walls of abstract geometrical shapes built of birch-faced plywood. They become a vertical, inhabitable landscape and a theatrical framing device for play.

The piece at the eastern end of the room can also be unfolded to form a partition allowing spaces in which the youngest children (infants up to two years old) can be quieter and more secluded.

In addition to this interior, the playgroup has a new rooftop playground, made of the same ply used on the interior and providing an external room for the children to have a sanctuary-like experience the city. Future phases include a plan for planted gazebos along the western side of this play area to provide sheltered areas for outdoor teaching.

The modest project was the last to be completed by Houlton Taylor as a partnership, which in 2002 split into Andrew Houlton Architects and Steven Taylor Architects.

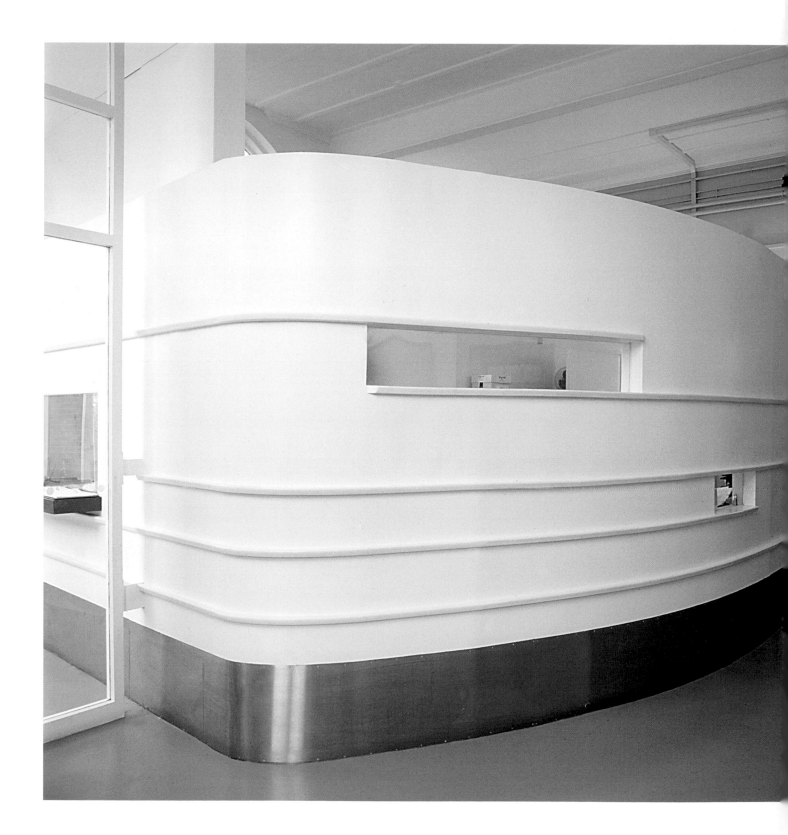

Stockwell Primary School, SW9
DSDHA

DSDHA is a young practice, based in unfashionable Elephant and Castle, that has used great tenacity to find a host of work in the education sector – traditionally one of the most difficult for young architects to break into. They are now designing a 315-place school in Sheffield and have completed two nurseries, one in Deptford and another in Bury, Lancashire.

This education work began with a project at a Victorian infants' and primary school in Stockwell, south London, which had severe problems with non-attendance and found it impossible to get parents in this deprived area of town interested in the running of the school.

The first phase of the project was tiny and simple – to give the school a new reception area and to rationalize the toilet provision. In response to this brief, on the face of it a short-term one, the architects devised a longer-term plan, trying to reorient the building towards the road and to give the whole institution, which was neglected by the community, some kind of connection with Stockwell.

The reception area consists of a white pod with good surveillance over the secure entrance and with windows cut into it at child and adult height. This very much reads as an element separate from the existing building, and has a material quality that provides an important marker of the ambitions of the school. Purple fluorescent light tubes, which are turned on out of school hours, give the school a certain intriguing presence at night.

Colour plays an important part in the design, with lime green poured-plastic floors in the toilets and coloured glass in the pods, all aiding orientation and providing some humorous visual interest among the heavy Victorian brick.

DSDHA's involvement has since grown to encompass a plan for a new school hall, which will provide the school with a 'shop front' to the street and complete the new axis suggested by the reception area. The work so far has rationalized circulation and servicing, and its quality has helped the school prove to parents that the school has ambition as an educational establishment.

Trinity College of Music, Greenwich, SE10
John McAslan + Partners

John McAslan has made a name for himself as one of the best in the business at remodelling historic buildings with sensitive but unashamedly modern designs. The Royal Naval College at Greenwich is part of a World Heritage Site and one of Britain's most important complexes of buildings, planned by Christopher Wren and Nicholas Hawksmoor and built between 1662 and 1769. The buildings have been altered and added to over the years and hardly suggested themselves as an obvious home for the Trinity College of Music, which moved into King Charles Court in 2002. McAslan was given the job of making the Grade 1 listed buildings work as a modern music school.

The original cellular layout had been altered by the Navy (unconstrained by heritage rules) and made into office space. Also, although the west wing has a reasonably simple corridor arrangement, the east was a complicated knot of public rooms and service areas. McAslan has reinstated original partition lines in many places, and has finished the whole interior in a reasonably neutral but hardwearing white render, with stone for the staircases.

Often, new fabric is emphatically expressed as separate from historic structures, such as in the practice rooms. These are heavily soundproofed boxes coloured red to reveal themselves as reversible contemporary additions. Other colours, such as yellow and blue, are used to show interventions and to mark out administration and service areas.

Acoustic engineer Arup was used for the practice rooms, but a modest budget meant that air-conditioning was not an option, so windows tend to be left open in the summer with resulting acoustic leakage. This is a pleasure for visitors wandering around the site, but probably less so for the practising student.

The decision of Trinity, one of Europe's most prestigious conservatoires, to move to Greenwich gives new life to these historic buildings, and the sound of practising musicians is a delight for visitor and student alike. McAslan's project is done with a light touch, yet feels identifiably contemporary.

Living

Anderson House, W1
Jamie Fobert Architects

The client for the Anderson house, a wealthy lawyer, endured a whole summer in a semi-derelict backlands warehouse near Oxford Circus just to see if he liked living in the area. He plumbed in a bath himself and settled down to live in garret-like surroundings. With such commitment to the project, it is little wonder that this has turned out to be one of the most remarkable new houses in the capital in recent years.

The Anderson House is a watershed project for architect Jamie Fobert and has had a lot of attention for a building that is very small. It won an RIBA award and the Manser Medal for best one-off house. It consists of just three main areas: the high and grand roof-lit living space; the modest timber-lined guest bedroom, which overlooks the living area; and the master bedroom, with its concrete bath and shower and its terrace. It is distinct from most contemporary houses in having a single line of circulation that never doubles back on itself and at no point allows you to read the entire arrangement of the house. Like a subterranean *promenade architecturale*, it consciously frames a set of views along a journey from one doorway to another.

This promenade begins from the front door, proceeds along a corridor, down a flight of stairs and then round a corner to the main living space. This slim corridor was the only access to the site during construction, and remains so now. The area does not feel like a basement, however, despite being strongly inward-looking.

This house, mainly because of its hemmed-in site, is resolutely contemplative. Its inwardness is turned to dramatic and beautiful effect, particularly in the views from the guest bedroom to the living-room. Looking from this very small bedroom through two layers of glass to the living area allows the suddenly close ceiling to take on the qualities of the sky (through reflections in the light-well) and, owing to the ripples in the concrete, those of a rumpled duvet.

Apartment, Hampstead, NW5
ARU/Florian Beigel/Philip Christou

Florian Beigel's work at the Architecture Research Unit at London Metropolitan University usually involves projects on a very large scale. In the past, the unit's work has included regenerating open-cast coal mines near Leipzig in Germany, planning a new publishing city in Korea, and giving new life to an old military installation in Berlin.

When it came to his own flat, though, Beigel was anxious to conform to the same principles that drive his larger-scale work. He has always stood for a style of planning that is radically against the overly deterministic models that drive much contemporary city development. His methods depend on a notion of 'landscape infrastructure', which establishes territories and areas without trying to design every architectural detail of a city. A key part of his work is to allow for chance and development over time. His ideas have made him one of the most influential teachers and practitioners in London.

The flat is, on a micro scale, a realization of these ideas. Set within a Victorian house on the edge of Hampstead Heath, the layout of rooms was re-established as originally intended, and all wall-mounted radiators replaced with underfloor heating. This established the capacity of the rooms, but also started to suggest the kind of flexibility that Beigel's work strives for. This theme is carried through to the kitchen in particular, which has no fixed fittings, but instead a series of stainless steel pieces that sit in the centre of the room, turning cooking into a social act and reinforcing the feeling of flexibility. The configuration of the rooms can be changed at any time, surely achieving Beigel's aim of a non-deterministic layout without resorting to an open-plan solution. The result makes full use of the generous proportions of the Victorian building.

An appealingly personal touch is the bedroom floor – a *hanji* paper floor imported from Korea, where Beigel has carried out a number of projects, and made from mulberry tree pulp soaked in resin. It is a beautiful material, with a real sense of delicacy and fineness that sublimates the ordinariness of paper. It is one of very few of its kind in the country.

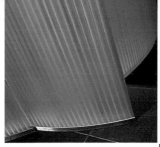

Beck penthouse, Docklands, E14
Richard Hywel Evans Architecture and Design

If you are going to do a residential interior this tasteless, you might as well do it with gusto. The Beck penthouse is in an ordinary new residential building in Docklands, for which the wealthy client wanted "an interior like none I've ever walked into". The result is the kind of interior a Bond villain might spend time in, updated for the twenty-first century.

The rise of men's style magazines in the UK has not really gone hand in hand with a rise in the style of men's clothes or surroundings; they've just got a little more shiny and expensive. This penthouse is the interior design version of *FHM* or *Loaded* magazine – the quintessential contemporary bachelor pad.

Entry is through a huge walnut-veneer door into an elliptical lounge. This has spectacular views, and the cladding of walls in stainless steel maximizes the room's natural light and provides a space-age setting for an integrated fish tank and (of course) plasma-screen TV. Recessed silk blinds can be pulled across at night.

Amoeboid shapes in the ceiling conceal services and lighting and reflect the curves of the furniture. The furniture is genuinely impressive, including a cast aluminium and walnut dining table supported on a single aluminium leg and surrounded by curved banquette seating. This updates the retro-futurism of the 1950s diner.

A spiral staircase, surrounded by exposed brick, leads up to the roof terrace (and Astroturf putting green), and a door through to the bedroom reveals that it's not all hyper-ventilating space-age design. It is curiously sober, with cream leather bedhead and pleated silk wall-hangings in beige. The wardrobe, opposite the bed, has full-height etched glass doors lit from behind.

It looks more like a bar than a flat in places, but one can only imagine that its owner would appreciate this more than most. Tremendous fun.

Courtnell Street house, Notting Hill, W2
Boyarsky Murphy Architects

The companion project to Boyarsky Murphy's house in
Hammersmith (see pages 168–69), this refurbishment of a
Victorian house in Notting Hill is another scheme based around a
spectacular staircase. This time, though, the circulation was the
basis of the project, with a brief from the client to divide the house
into two – a private and public face for the residence.

This was achieved by retaining an existing staircase at the
front of the house, and adding a subtle new stair at the back,
made of painted steel with timber treads. This is accommodated
in a minimal glass extension accessed through folding doors
on the ground floor. Rising up this new staircase, you end up at
the elaborate TV and music room, with custom-installed sound
system and a long bench, upholstered in blue, running the length
of the room.

There is a constant play in the house between single- and
double-height volumes. The extension at the back is double
height, and a second double-height space is created between the
second and third floors, with a bed housed in a sleeping pod at
third-floor level and bathroom and dressing areas beneath. Also,
underneath the pod are an enclosed study and a door leading to
a guest bedroom.

Reserved timber and render are the principal materials
downstairs, along with full-height metallic fabric drapes at the
window. Upstairs, the pod-like mezzanine adds more organic form,
its concrete and plaster-covered plywood curves lit indirectly, and
the heavy-pile carpet that adds to the luxury.

If the contrast between polished plaster curves and the
Victorian order of the rest of the house jars in some moments,
Boyarsky Murphy's sure touch is undeniable.

Eaton House penthouses, Canary Wharf, E14
Walters & Cohen

Grappling with the problem of how to distinguish one set of characterless apartments from another exercises many of the minds that engage with the strange built environment of Canary Wharf. Walters & Cohen had as their context one of the slightly more characterful parts of the Wharf: Canary Riverside. This development is by commercial architect Koetter Kim in collaboration with Philippe Starck, who brought some interest to the scheme with a quite extraordinary copper roof on the Four Seasons Hotel.

Walters & Cohen carried out the Holmes Place health club at the development in 2000, and then took on the job of designing six luxury apartments for Canary Riverside Development.

The open-plan apartments have been designed with double-height spaces and mezzanine floors. A palette of natural materials has been used throughout, including light and dark limestone, wool carpets, Carrara marble, granite, and solid oak floors with underfloor heating in every room.

The most individual part of the scheme is in fact a piece of appliqué. The architect commissioned architectural photographer Hélène Binet to produce images of the river and superimposed them on the walls of two of the apartments alongside their glass staircases. Binet, a legendary London-based photographer who has worked with such architects as Zaha Hadid and Daniel Libeskind, photographed the receding tide of the Thames and the retaining wall along the embankment. These images were then blown up to the size of the wall to give an alternative view of the river within the penthouse, juxtaposed with the actual views through the windows.

The viewer experiences these images at various scales, from close up while on the stair, and from further away when on the other side of the living and dining area. As a way of beginning to suggest an identity for an area commonly held to have none, it impresses.

House for an art collector, Chelsea, SW3
Tony Fretton Architects/Mark Pimlott

Architect Tony Fretton and artist Mark Pimlott are long-time friends and collaborators, and this house – the Red House, as it is commonly known, on account of its deep red masonry exterior – is their most in-depth project yet. It was Pimlott who introduced Fretton to the client, a very wealthy and prominent art collector, and a collaboration took shape that involved artist, architect and client in one of the most remarkable residential interiors in London.

Pimlott's involvement extends to designing everything from balustrades to bathrooms to door handles, each one treated as its own piece of artwork. His installations are not just applied decoration, though. The main reception room, for example, accommodates the client's extraordinary collection of art, and therefore required gallery-quality lighting. To hide this, Pimlott created slashes in the ceiling soffit, creating sensuous undulations that are almost imperceptible due to the undifferentiated colour scheme.

In the Miesian dining-room, Pimlott again concentrated on the soffit, hanging an acoustic panel of fabric from the ceiling and hand painting a grid of squares with an oil stick. This was a process that took eight weeks to complete, and the result is very beautiful indeed. Other rooms treated in this holistic manner include the day-lit, white-tiled bathroom and the wonderful downstairs lavatory, which has been wallpapered with a large-scale printed image of a night sky.

Perhaps the most beautiful of all Pimlott's contributions is in the hallway. The hall is proportionally grand, but materially modest, punctuated only by the sculptural steel balustrade, which is strangely contradictory in its classical proportions and industrial material.

There are moments of eccentricity, too, such as the exposed concrete ceiling in the bedroom that refers to the client's childhood home – a house by Modernist legend and National Theatre architect Denys Lasdun. Pimlott is to continue working on furniture and other interior pieces for the house, meaning that this wonderful place will remain a work in progress. It's just a shame that we members of the public will never get to see it.

House, Tantallon Road, Balham, SW12
Dow Jones Architects

This project, by up-and-coming practice Dow Jones (based in south London), is another variation on the conversion of a Victorian house of the type that occupies many young architects' time. Here the architects were hired to remodel and extend the ground floor of the house, which, unusually for the era in which it was built, had the kitchen in the middle of the floorplan. This arrangement suited the family, and they wanted to retain it, but also to extend the back of the house to provide more space.

This approach inevitably led to the kitchen becoming landlocked, with no external walls and thus no natural light or ventilation. Dow Jones's response was to create an extension that made the new dining-room the focus. This was lined almost entirely – floors, walls and soffits – in oak. The light and wood radiate from this room, and connect, conceptually and physically, the three new rooms. The dining-room has a roof-light in one corner, shared by the kitchen, which allows daylight to spill down one wall, differentiating the otherwise consistent material of the room.

The family room at the back of the plan is divided from the dining-room by a large piece of oak-veneered furniture, which incorporates storage. The oak flooring continues through to the garden behind the house.

The choice of oak directly relates to the client's desire to decorate the house with a range of objects and pictures. The oiled oak responds dynamically to natural light, both absorbing and reflecting, and this effect is magnified when it is used on every available surface.

House, Blythe Road, Hammersmith, W14
Boyarsky Murphy

Refurbishing the interiors of Victorian houses for wealthy clients is a staple of the young architect and interior designer. Many of these projects are kept towards the back of designers' portfolios, as most lapse into a good-taste approximation of contemporary design.

Nicholas Boyarsky and Nicola Murphy, however, have quickly become masters of this type, and have completed a number of projects that show inventiveness, lateral thinking and a subtly dramatic touch. When approached to design an extension to a terraced house in Hammersmith, the pair decided to start with the shell of the building, stripping away all spine walls and the stairwell. A new steel structure in the party wall enabled all three floors to be open plan. The new structure also allowed for an extraordinary new cantilevered open-tread staircase that extends, in one flight, from the ground to the second floor, with a fork at the first floor leading to the study and office area. The continuous staircase becomes a space in itself, giving a 9 m (30 ft) floor to ceiling height.

The staircase amounts to a dramatic piece of sculpture in what is now a very minimal space. It is enhanced by the choice of rich materials – quarter-sawn oak treads, powder-coated steel stanchions and leather-covered handrails – showing that the architects have not stopped with a defining spatial statement, but have continued their attention into the details. The quality of materials in the bedrooms is of a similarly high standard: leather covers the floors and European walnut is used for the custom-made storage cupboards and bookcases.

The drama continues upstairs, with the bathroom suspended over the void created by the stair. The shower cubicle is made of photochromic glass, meaning that it can change from opaque to clear at the flick of a switch, giving views down through the house from the shower. This is somewhat gimmicky, but a nice twist on the John Pawson-inspired trend for providing showers with skylights to the exterior. Here the views connect the bather with the rest of the house, rather than with external elements.

A new basement was built to provide a guest bedroom, utility room and storage space, making this, in all, a spatially generous, opulent two-bedroom live/work building. The design of the interior has been thought out sensitively and a careful prioritization has paid dividends. The client did not place the kitchen high on the list of priorities, for example, and Boyarsky Murphy was able to economize, placing hob, sink and other utilities in a simple white island towards the front of the ground-floor living space. This allowed funds to be spent on the serious underpinning required for the basement (all work in the basement had to be carried out

by hand, as there was no way to bring machinery into the space), and on the steel structure in the party wall, as well as keeping the material specification high throughout.

House, Hampstead, NW5
Spence Harris Hogan Associates

There are times when the judicious use of a single beautiful material can transform a space from four walls into a room. And then there are times when, however many sumptuous materials you throw at it, a room comes out looking like a middle-market hotel.

SHH, faced with a £1,000,000 budget to transform a Victorian house in Hampstead from flats into a single family house, have made something that should be luxurious, but in fact looks as though it is trying a little too hard.

The architects came up with a completely new internal layout for the house, ripping out bathrooms, replacing most of the flooring and inserting a new internal 'feature' staircase, which now runs from the lower-ground garden level to the second floor.

The entrance is a huge walnut door measuring 2.5 x 1.6 m (8 x 5 ft) that leads through an internal porch with matted flooring to a further walnut door. Beyond this is the main entrance lobby tiled with pieces of limestone 60 cm (2 ft) square. The grand staircase, with its bizarre flame-themed balustrade, is then in full view. The overweening bespoke nature of the stair is echoed in the reception room, which features a walnut border to the flooring and a walnut table 3 m (10 ft) long. One wall of this room is a full-height glass wall looking out over the double-height void above the lower-ground-floor breakfast room (with B&B Italia kitchen) and onto the rear garden beyond.

The bathroom on the ground floor has upholstered suede walls, as does the master bedroom, which, rather than having a door, has a pivoting section of wall that accentuates the enclosed interior of this adult space.

There are moments of quite beautiful interior design here, but they occur mainly when the architect is not trying to do too much. The living-room has a retro feel that is quite amusing, with its restored original chandelier, etched glass door, timber parquet and white rug. However, the kind of family that needs a dumb waiter (as in this house) is probably not the kind of family that enjoys a minimal, contemporary approach to design.

House and studio, Liverpool Road, N1
DRDH Architects

This Georgian house and shopfront in Islington nearly ended up condemned when DRDH first came to the job. Its cheap Georgian construction had been hugely compromised by the previous owners, who had removed much of the brick underpinning in the basement. Added to this, a stream running beneath the site threatened to cause the house to collapse before it could be rebuilt. It was rescued, however, and became a superb calling card for this up-and-coming practice.

The existing house was long and thin, and had to accommodate a home and a studio for the client's arts company. This is housed in the basement, which has its own front door and can be reached from the street by a staircase descending through a double-height space at the front of the house. The ground floor contains the main living area and kitchen, and the top floor is the bedroom and bathroom.

The dominant feature is the concrete that forms an element on every floor – the new foundation, the south wall of the basement and ground floor, and a screen for the bathroom on the top floor. This concrete is beautifully cast, left raw and unpolished, with the marks of the Douglas fir shuttering still clearly preserved. The timber used for many of the other surfaces in the interior is also Douglas fir, in the same proportions as the shuttering that contained the concrete as it was poured.

There is a pleasing play of scale and view in the house. It is possible to see from front to back, but the balustrade means that the living area becomes more private, and the change of level for the kitchen at the rear hides this part of the house from the view of the street. This graded intimacy is aided by screens, which can be closed to separate the house from the studio and street completely.

Upstairs is just one space, divided by curtains pleated to the same dimensions as the timber panels – a reference to the open arrangement of houses in the West Indies, the client's childhood home. This space also leads out onto a terrace, a sheer surface of timber punctured by the roof-light that looks down on the living area.

Private residence, St John's Wood, NW8
Eric Parry Architects

Eric Parry's work is a testament to his ability to work at a range of different scales and still express a very clear architectural ethos. Parry trained at the Architectural Association and the Royal College of Art, but it is with Cambridge University that his work has become associated – he studied for his MA there and taught design at the architecture school for fourteen years. His portfolio is increasing in size all the time, and the practice was nominated for the Stirling Prize in 2003 for an office building on Finsbury Square.

Despite this leap in scale of late, Parry is an immensely cultured architect and he has had a long association with the art world. This house in St John's Wood is for a classic Parry client – educated and with a hugely impressive collection of contemporary art and modern and contemporary furniture. The brief was to provide a spacious house that could suit the life of a family with five young children, while also being able to accommodate major pieces of art and furniture.

When a large nineteenth-century house was found in St John's Wood, it was stripped of a host of additions, including a lift shaft, partitions and a pool. The form of the original house was re-established, and a new extension the full width of the site was added to provide a sequence of generous, well-lit spaces for both formal entertaining and family life. These are finished in natural and hardwearing materials such as stone and timber for floors, and selected elements are finished with stainless steel, glass, lacquer and horsehair panels.

Each room in the extension has full-height frameless windows, establishing a strong relationship with the garden, which was designed by award-winning landscape architect Christopher Bradley-Hole. The ground-floor extension was built with a steel frame to allow for large, uninterrupted spaces, and solid, expansive walls allow for lots of storage and provide drama when one enters the rooms.

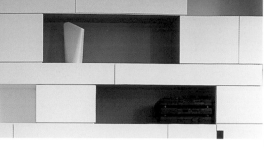

House, Stockwell Park Crescent, SW9
David Mikhail

David Mikhail has been a much talked about name in architecture for some years. He won the high-profile housing competition Europan in 1991 at the age of twenty-eight, and seven years later he was still young enough to come second in the Young Architect of the Year award. Still relatively young for an architect, he has carried out a series of very cool and stylish domestic projects that display his love of a limited palette of quality materials and open and transparent plans.

A breakthrough project for Mikhail, his commission to convert a previously down-at-heel but listed Georgian house in Stockwell was won in a mini-competition with four other young practices. Mikhail reinstated the external envelope of the 1830s house, apart from the spectacular double-height glazed door he installed to provide light and views out from the main living spaces. This huge sliding door provides interest inside, too, and its proportions are echoed in the doors (which are around 3 m [10 ft] high in places) between the hallway and living-room.

Mikhail laid an external timber deck that continues from outside, through the hallway and into the living spaces. This forms a coherent surface from which new elements, such as the steel and glass stairway to the first floor, can rise.

Mikhail also designed furniture and storage for the house, designed to fit the owners' extensive collections of records and films. These form discrete elements in the space, revealing the architect's sympathy for a European Modernist aesthetic, particularly the de Stijl art of Mondrian and van Doesburg.

The house is for a family with young children, and Mikhail has provided a communal children's room that will eventually be divided into individual bedrooms, but for now serves as a huge open-plan playspace, with furniture pushed to the sides of the room.

House for Dinos Chapman, Fashion Street, E1
Brinkworth

The gentrification that has transformed east London in the last ten years has often been characterized as a process that began with artists moving to Shoreditch, Hoxton and Spitalfields, and that ended with an influx of rich kids on the lookout for a slice of credibility, displacing the creative community.

In Spitalfields, it is the artists themselves who have gentrified. On the back of the success brought by the 1990s Britart explosion, many have forsaken their original draughty warehouse spaces for something more befitting their circumstances. In Spitalfields, residents still include Tracey Emin, Gilbert and George and Chris Ofili, who lives on Fashion Street next door to those *enfants terribles* of British art, Jake and Dinos Chapman.

Multi-award-winning Brinkworth was voted in 2002 one of the top ten interior designers of the decade, and mixing the practice with one of the most famous figures in British art is an exciting cocktail. This scheme is surprisingly polite, given Chapman's reputation as one of the most controversial figures in British art. The project is a refurbishment of a five-storey Victorian property on Fashion Street, an agglomeration of nondescript office and retail spaces that Chapman wanted to convert into a family house. He wanted to allow for the maximum possible visual connectivity between the spaces, which are occupied by Chapman, his partner, Tiphaine De Lussy, and their two children.

Brinkworth conceived the project as a gradual excavation of spaces for habitation linked by a staircase that leads up through half-landings and mezzanines and extends the whole height of the house. Spaces include a balcony-like study 'pulpit' for the children and a 52 sq m (560 sq ft) playroom. The playroom, a white box room, is lit by a trough in the floor that can be controlled to change its colour.

The internal finishes are diverse, ranging from timber, rubber and terrazzo flooring to Formica and iroko for furniture. Rather than trying to turn itself into a piece of art, the house responds well to the needs of a family with two young children.

Show flat at The Jam Factory, Bermondsey, SE1
Minus One Architects

The Jam Factory, a 1901 Hartley's preserves factory in Bermondsey reworked in 2003 by Ian Simpson Architects, is the latest boutique housing development in London to reinhabit a grand but decaying industrial building. Just the thing for the increasing demand for a taste of raw loft living.

The scheme by Minus One Architects comes from a series of options for the flats' buyers, with others devised by such up-and-coming designers as Softroom, Azman Owens and Mayer Vuska. Design has been used here to help draw buyers to an area of London that, although rapidly gentrifying, is hardly in the league of Shoreditch or Borough in the regeneration stakes.

Minus One's project is more like a piece of furniture than a lining for an apartment. To preserve the feel of an industrial space, the accommodation for the kitchen, bathroom and storage are arranged into a central cube, with apertures cut into it to create functional areas.

The upper layer of the cube contains long-term storage cupboards, creating a kind of loft that takes advantage of the space above the flats' suspended ceilings. The bottom layer is for everyday storage, and the middle layer, distinguished by its reflective and transparent materials, contains the openings that form the bathroom and kitchen. Despite the cube's diagrammatic appearance, it is materially rich enough to feel more satisfying than this, creating intriguing effects of solid and void, allowing some views through glazed areas and screening off others.

These are not quite the raw shells that someone from the meatpacking district of Manhattan might prefer as their lofts, but there is no doubt that this is one of more successful attempts at providing solutions for apartments in capsule form.

10 Palace Gate, Kensington, SW7
John McAslan + Partners

John McAslan's reputation as one of the finest restorers of Modern Movement buildings in the UK has been enhanced by his wonderful restoration of Mendelsohn and Chermayeff's De La Warr Pavilion in Bexhill-on-Sea and his reworking of the Peter Jones department store in Chelsea (see pages 94–95). Palace Gate is a work by Modern Movement scion Wells Coates, whose Lawn Road flats in Hampstead were recently the subject of a long and high-profile preservation battle and are now under sympathetic ownership.

Wells Coates's building on Palace Gate in Kensington is the least high profile of his three major new-build works (the other two being Lawn Road and Embassy Court). This may be because the microflat configuration of Lawn Road became obsolete and the inappropriate construction details of Embassy Court led to structural failures, while Palace Gate had always done its job pretty well. However, as is so common in this country, alterations made in the 1960s to the 1939 building had destroyed the attributes of the original plan, and other architectural details had been removed over time.

John McAslan + Partners' phased approach began with the detailed restoration of the building's lobby. The main moves were to remove 1960s additions and as far as possible reinstate the Wells Coates plan. This avoids a traditional axial plan with formal reception in favour of a more free-flowing and dynamic progression through the ground floor. The project grew into a comprehensive restoration, which included the retention of the sculptural glazed stair and lift tower that connects the two blocks of the complex. This means that the building, on the curve of Palace Gate, remains highly visible from the road.

The fit-out also extends to furnishing the reception area with Modernist classic furniture and lighting, with identifiably contemporary timber screens forming a new backdrop.

McAslan has been careful not to become pigeon-holed as a restoration architect, also taking on major new-build and masterplanning projects, but his rigorous research into the architects of high Modernism make him one of the most sensitive interpreters of these architects' original intentions.

Price residence, Chiswick, W4
51%

Like wife-swapping, modern design in the Victorian suburbs of London is something that usually stays behind closed doors. Those gracious red-brick façades can sometimes hide a hotbed of contemporary design replacing the Laura Ashley.

This Chiswick house was reinstated as a family residence after it had been divided into flats. The job of rearranging it into one that would allow the client to accommodate their two children, to throw regular parties and to suit their collection of contemporary furniture fell to 51%, a Clerkenwell-based architecture practice founded in 1995 by South African Catherine du Toit and Peter Thomas. This much-praised small practice is making a name for itself with a series of sensitive interventions in existing buildings.

Key to the rearrangement was a central corridor, for which 51% conceived a long, large piece of cabinetry that provided storage, but could also conceal connecting doors. This means that the space can be open or subdivided, depending on the requirements. The materials used, including oak for the floor and cherry for the cabinets and panelling, connect conceptually all the spaces of the ground floor, while serving as a backdrop for displaying the client's collection of glass in illuminated recesses.

Fittings, too, are uncompromisingly contemporary, and reflect the client's collecting instincts – coloured pod lamps by Ross Lovegrove being particularly prominent.

The house is reworked, too, as a Janus, with the conservative Victorian façade giving no hint of the glassy and contemporary back, which opens up views of the garden from the ground floor. It also provides oversize sliding doors and glazed openings in the roof.

Loft for a writer, Soho, W1
Richard Hywel Evans Architecture and Design

Although Richard Hywel Evans's work has largely been in the residential and commercial sectors, it is for an office building – the spectacular new-build Cellular Operations HQ in Swindon – that he is best known. It is no surprise, then, that this loft, the Soho home of a TV producer and a Booker Prize-nominated author, shows as much flair in the work spaces as it does in the more domestic environments.

The 300 sq m (3230 sq ft) apartment is over three floors of an ex-industrial building, with balconies giving spectacular views over London. The pieces of furniture take on this industrial aesthetic, albeit in a much sanitized manner, through the use of stainless and galvanized steel as the principal materials, along with rubber in places, all set on a light-timber floor.

The spaces are dominated by the writer's vast collection of books, which are housed in immense steel-faced bookcases with black backgrounds and glass shelves. The facings act as frames, displaying and making coherent the array of different spines.

The two workstations were custom-designed. The TV producer's desktop is of blue etched glass, supported on a triangular stainless steel set of drawers, with curved edges fitting beneath the amoeba shape of the desk. Surrounding shelves and cupboards take on the language of the bookshelves outside, but are inset with etched glass panels backlit with coloured lights.

The writer's room is on a mezzanine above the main living-room, with access to the bookshelves from a ladder on sliding castors.

The focus is not just on work, though: the loft boasts a movable bar made of stainless steel, with integrated ice bucket and serving tray, that can be moved on castors from the dining area to the sofas after dinner.

TC House, Belsize Park, NW3
6a Architects

The conversion of a Georgian terraced house for a client with a very limited budget is the definition of a young architect's project. Almost every new practice gets at least one, and the lucky are the architects who leave behind a world of tasteful plasterboard fit-outs and glassy extensions before their forties.

6a Architects has succeeded, but even this early project showed their willingness to try to move beyond the generic contemporary residential interior despite limited means. The client works in the music industry, and wanted to convert this Georgian house, situated on Quadrant Grove in Belsize Park, into a place in which to live and work. The project consisted of opening up the ground floor of the house, and adding a new single-storey bathroom and kitchen extension to the rear.

The architect sees the house as a series of open rooms moving in an enfilade from street to garden. Revealed sections of the original house give a sense of the building's scale and arrangement before the redesign. A long, low, wooden bench is the unifying element, which changes its form as you move through the house. Initially, the timber continues up the wall to provide storage behind. In the second room, the bench continues without this raised section, and finally, in the garden room at the back, it metamorphoses into two free-standing benches. The bench performs the function of storing the client's huge record collection out of sight, and the new timber complements the black painted timber floor well.

Although the project is simple, it hints at a set of architectural concerns that found fuller expression in 6a's Oki-Ni boutique on Savile Row (see pages 90–91). These suggest the potential for large-scale pieces of furniture to become architectural elements in existing spaces. 6a has since made some impressive shortlists, and will no doubt be testing these ideas on a bigger scale soon.

Lasheras studio, Shoreditch, N1
Simon Conder

Simon Conder is one of Britain's most profound, and modest, architects. His career has run the gamut from prodigy – he had a piece of furniture put into production at the tender age of sixteen – to heading up a large-scale office, back to a studio of around five or six, and producing bespoke projects of immense quality that mine an interest in abstracted vernacular forms and simple materials.

His interior design projects are very recognizable, often employing with great ingenuity the birch-faced plywood that has become something of a trademark (his Barbieri apartment and the interior to his Dungeness house are two examples). This fit-out, which occupies a warehouse building in north London, was produced for the photographer José Lasheras and is one of the most elegant ways of dealing with a warehouse space that has been seen in recent years. It achieves the elusive goal of dealing stylishly with living and working in the same space.

The design essentially consists of two pods built of plywood that can be moved at will around the otherwise uninterrupted space. The boxes are entitled 'Dry' and 'Wet', according to the services they contain. The 'Wet' box incorporates a small kitchen built into one side, and contains a shower, basin and toilet. Water and waste pipes can be plugged into one of three positions in the apartment, and an in-built macerator allows small-diameter waste pipes to be used. The 'Dry' box consists of two parts that can be swung apart to reveal an office and storage area and accommodates a sleeping deck on top.

The extreme level of flexibility that this solution provides allows the studio to be rented out to other photographers or used as a guest flat, according to the layout. It also allows the existing space to be read as one volume and is a hugely cost-effective way of dealing with the ubiquitous loft shell. It also shows Conder's ingenuity and reveals how his furniture-making past contributes to his architecture today.

Working

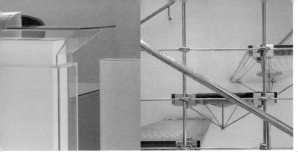

AMEC headquarters, Clerkenwell, EC1
Eva Jiricna

AMEC is a rather untrendy multi-disciplinary construction firm, not known for its cutting-edge building design. But when it commissioned an architect to fit out its corporate headquarters in a refurbished warehouse in Clerkenwell, it chose a practice that knows how to deliver a sense of occasion to an interior.

Eva Jiricna is a Czech émigrée who has been based in London for over thirty years. She has been involved in some of the most influential interiors ever designed in the capital, including the Lloyds building (while working for Richard Rogers Partnership) and the Way In store at Harrods, which she designed with Future Systems founder Jan Kaplicky. She has since stuck fast to a highly machined aesthetic, but has taken this in a more delicate direction than most British high-tech architects, such as Nicholas Grimshaw or Norman Foster.

The fit-out for AMEC displays one of Jiricna's calling cards – the glass-and-steel staircase. These are something of a speciality of the practice, and the stair devised for AMEC is one of her most pleasing – a filigree steel mesh running down the middle of the staircase, from which are hung slender glass treads. An internal skylight allows daylight from the roof-terrace window to spill down the stairwell, and wall lights spiral down the wall, culminating in a rim of LEDs at the base.

The other showpiece is the reception desk, which is made entirely from bonded glass and lit from its base in the limestone floor. Jiricna's experiments with glass are, for her, an expression of her interests in architecture. "You can shape it, curve it, draw on it, cast it," she says; "you can transmit daylight, artificial light. It reflects, diffuses. It can control the environment." Her faith in glass has led to some of the most compelling technological experiments to be seen anywhere, and a host of awards for her and her practice.

Audi Forum, Piccadilly, W1
ITC concepts/Thomas Erikssons

ITC concepts can be said to be firmly at the more commercial end of interior design. They specialize in interior refurbishment for corporate clients, and tend to mention when they advertise that their work is always on time and on budget. Theirs is not design to make the heart beat faster, and the spatial configurations of their projects are only really interesting in the sense that they perform certain commercial functions efficiently and effectively.

It is fascinating that while some luxury marques, such as Prada, will employ the highest-profile architects possible to deliver buildings to embody their brand values, others, in this case Audi, will employ low-profile commercial architects to create their vision. What they have in common is the desire to create a presence that is more than just a retail outlet. The Piccadilly Audi showroom, or Forum, as it is known, opened at the beginning of 2002 with great fanfare and a spectacular lightshow. It is the sixth store of its type in the world, and now the concept is being rolled out to Paris, Munich, Stockholm, Madrid and New York.

The forum, which occupies a unit that used to be Canon's showroom, is intended as a conference venue, internet café and exhibition space, and to this end it lets the exhibits – the cars – speak for themselves. Rather than putting design in the face of the visitor, ITC stripped the interior down to its bare essentials: new mechanical and electrical services were installed behind specialist suspended ceilings, they plastered and partitioned the space, and they laid a ceramic-tiled floor. This all provides the perfect backdrop, which is never likely to overpower the cars.

The one piece of showmanship is the giant LED wall behind the glass-and-steel staircase, which can be altered and changed to suit the way the space is being used.

Bartle Bogle Hegarty office, Soho, W1
Urban Salon

BBH is one of the coolest of the big West End advertising agencies, but its quirky branding, which features sheep prominently, had never been backed up by its premises. Although well located near Carnaby Street, they had the kind of generic landlord's interior that is familiar to most office workers.

On signing a new lease, BBH appointed Urban Salon, a young Southwark-based architecture practice, to give the office a new identity and reconfigure the space to accommodate 100 extra employees. In order to differentiate zones in the three-storey office, Urban Salon used a riot of different materials, finishes, furniture and colours to define social areas, work spaces and meeting rooms.

The most immediately spectacular space is the reception area, set at the foot of an atrium. Above the main desk a distended black fabric soffit with a magenta panel hovers directly over the head of the receptionist. Expressive ceilings are used elsewhere, too (translucent blue ceiling tiles cluster around social spaces). Other prominent surfaces include the boldly striped floors, Snowcrash-designed acoustic panels in the café, translucent blue partitions for meeting rooms and natural timber for benches and some other furniture pieces.

Most of the agency's 400 staff spend a lot of their time out of the office and a hot-desking system is used. Research areas, though, needed to be quieter and calmer, and custom-designed tables with leather tops add a note of luxury. The whole project has had a huge amount of time and a huge number of ideas lavished on it, from the clever timber furniture, with circular apertures to contain rolled-up newspapers and magazines, to the acoustic separation of the café and working areas. The practice has had a reputation as up-and-coming for some years, and this project goes some way to demonstrating its potential.

Bloomberg European headquarters, Finsbury Square, EC2
Powell Tuck Associates

Fitting out a Norman Foster building is an intimidating task for any architect. Powell Tuck's fit-out of Foster's 2000 building on Finsbury Square gets around the problem by identifying clearly with the occupier – business information giant Bloomberg – rather than being too precious about who the architect of the original building was.

When Bloomberg acquired the lease to the building in 2000, they also decided to upgrade their existing HQ – the adjoining City Gate House, constructed in 1928 as a gentleman's club and designed by F.R. Gould with Sir Giles Gilbert Scott. The two buildings' rather polite façades conceal an interior that reflects the information obsession of Bloomberg, in all its headache-inducing glory.

On entering, there is a two-storey glass atrium from which neon-lit escalators lead to the first-floor reception and the staff restaurant. On the way up, a digital ticker and an array of screens start the information bombardment. This is continued in the restaurant, where cylindrical columns house more screens. The restaurant is the only place to eat in the building, and all food is free, encouraging employees to mix and meet in this centrally located space.

The Bladerunner aesthetic continues into the soaring atrium, with its bridges and more neon that colour-codes each floor. On the ground floor there is a gallery (which can be also accessed from the street) and a series of lecture rooms and auditoriums that are used for Bloomberg's extensive arts programme.

The historic City Gate House is a much more solid and conventional masonry building, and the architect took the decision to put the TV studios here to benefit from the poorer lighting conditions. As in the newer offices, there are many information-inspired light installations, such as an LED wall that shows the silhouettes of those entering and leaving the building – a perfect representation of Bloomberg's slightly sinister corporate mix of surveillance, management, control and dissemination of information.

Braxton office, Smithfields, EC1
Harper Mackay

Management consultancies are companies that, by and large, tell other firms what to do to sort out their problems, so it is always interesting to see how they communicate something about themselves to designers and architects. Braxton – formerly part of Deloitte Consulting – found itself in exactly this position when it commissioned Harper Mackay to fit out its 14,000 sq m (150,000 sq ft) of offices near the Barbican.

The building, designed by EPR Architects, was under construction when Harper Mackay was appointed to the job, and they were able to influence decisions about the size of the atrium and how open the office floors would be, electing to maximize natural light into the office areas. Beyond this, the fit-out takes swatches of colour and adds them to a bland office interior, making for some genuinely satisfying moments.

One's first encounter is with the giant, appallingly named 'branding blade', a curving sheet of glass with integrated screens and LEDs under its surface that can be switched to different colours. This is allowed to be the dominant visual element, with classy cream terrazzo for the floor and reception desk. Beyond this is a tiny forest of reed-like orange cylinders, which act as a screen. As is characteristic of Harper Mackay's work, a large graphic mural adds another layer of decoration, which can be seen at close quarters as you ascend in the lift.

On the office floors themselves are the usual glass-clad meeting rooms, as well as pods for coffee-making and photocopying. Demountable elements create informal break-out and meeting spaces on every floor.

All of this is embellished with well-chosen furniture, which eschews the staid Barcelona chairs of many corporate atriums and opts instead for a playful mix of Starck, Castiglioni and George Nelson, among others. In all, this could have been a great deal more corporate than it is, and it forms a good illustration of what can be done with a blue-chip client willing to take one or two risks.

Bulo showroom and office, Shad Thames, SE1
Brinkworth

This showroom and office in Shad Thames for Belgian design retailer Bulo shows interior designer Adam Brinkworth's chameleon-like ability to tune into the values of his clients and create spaces sympathetic to them. Although Brinkworth made his name with a succession of retail interiors (over sixty fit-outs for Karen Millen and a retail concept for Whistles [see pages 100–101] among others), the practice was always keen to diversify into workplaces. It found the perfect partner in Bulo, which called for an interior sympathetic to the design sensibility of its native Flanders, home to such coolly minimal designers as Maarten van Severen.

Brinkworth was originally employed to fit out a floor of this luxury residential building as a speculative office development, but the brief changed when Bulo took over the space as a showroom and office.

The interior achieves a luxurious warehouse aesthetic cheaply and humorously. The flooring is simply blockwork, varnished to give it a rich finish. This is mirrored, literally, by the ceiling, where the concrete soffit has been coated in a highly reflective resin, increasing the perceived ceiling height. The exposed ducting forms a network of silver and gold pipework spreading out across the ceiling. The cheap finishes mean that the building will reflect use – the floor will be worn away by people walking over it – but this is seen as an advantage, and takes the interior away from the pristine white-box shop interiors more commonly associated with furniture stores.

Walls are also left as raw blockwork, but white rendered boxes around the windows and covered columns reflecting light mean that the space is not totally raw. Minimally detailed glowing light-boxes complete the effect. Simple plywood furniture complements the completed showroom, which has an informality about it – a certain ambiguity between shopping environment and workplace.

five headquarters reception, Covent Garden, WC2
Buckley Gray

Launched in 1997, Channel 5 is the youngest of the terrestrial
television channels, but already saw the need for a comprehensive
rebranding exercise in September 2002. The channel changed its
name to the monosyllabic 'five' and employed young London-
based architect Buckley Gray to refurbish its head office, which is
situated on Long Acre in Covent Garden.

Working with creative strategists Walker Bannister Buss, design
agency Spin and advertising agency TBWA, Buckley Gray conceived
a design that provided practical improvements as well as a
presence on the street that reinforced the channel's new image.

The refurbishment of the reception minimizes the impact of
deliveries and heightens security, while still creating a shop
window to the street. Inside, an open reception area creates a
dialogue between the reception itself, the waiting area and the
street beyond. A black glass wall containing plasma screens with
backlit surrounds provides a backdrop to the reception desk, and
incorporates a one-way viewing window into a separate corridor
for deliveries. The reception is finished with minimal glass tables
at a low level and classic Modernist chairs, with the new logo in
supergraphics on one wall.

The redesign, though small, forms a key part of the channel's
public face. Buckley Gray has since gone on to design other
excellent interiors, including Northburgh House, an innovative
office space carved out of a disused loading bay in Clerkenwell.
The practice is now beginning to receive larger commissions,
including the redesign for the headquarters of the British Council
in Milan.

Claydon Heeley Jones Mason office, Battersea, SW11
Ushida Findlay

Ushida Findlay made its name with a series of intriguing and highly unconventional houses in Japan, including their Soft and Hairy and Truss Wall houses. The partnership has now divided, and partner Kathryn Findlay has based herself in London permanently, but the interest in strongly non-orthogonal geometries and unashamedly sensuous forms continues.

Their fit-out for advertising and marketing firm Claydon Heeley Jones Mason is over five floors of an undistinguished 1980s office block, and was completed on an extremely tight budget. The architect therefore persuaded the client to forsake the normal corporate cocktail of pricey but conservative materials and classic furniture for an approach that uses cheaper materials – PVC, mild steel, rubber and laminated mdf – thus stretching the budget to a bespoke interior.

The most striking area of the fit-out is the reception, which is bedecked in rolled steel ribbons that twist and bend through the space, dipping to form bench seats, and rising to form the mounts for screens. Coloured orange (the corporate colour of the firm) and silver (referencing the Thames flowing just outside, apparently), these form a dynamic badge for the company and are visible from the street outside.

The fit-out of the office spaces is highly pragmatic. CHJM wanted an office that could accommodate growing and shrinking teams, while allowing break-out meeting spaces to be as informal as possible. The architects arranged the office on a flexible grid grouped around six-person desk clusters and designed meeting spaces that do not require people to sit in an ordered way around large tables.

The space is detailed and arranged, as far as possible, without hierarchy, in an attempt to democratize the working environment. Material quality is maintained throughout, and the continuous blue rubber flooring melts into the sky when it reaches the glazed envelope of the building.

Dive Architects Studio, The Jam Factory, Bermondsey, SE1
Dive Architects

Dive Architects are a young practice whose work up until now has mostly consisted of very able interior fit-outs. However, partners Andy Nettleton and Ia Hjärre have also found a way of making projects for themselves by fitting out their own home and studio.

For their first project they made a family apartment out of a former potato warehouse near Borough Market, using a palette of muted greens and greys. Their most recent scheme has been to move their own office into a new studio in The Jam Factory, an ex-industrial building recently converted into flats and live/work space by Ian Simpson Architects (see also pages 180–81).

Dive took a two-floor shell and proceeded to covert it into an office that they could operate from and a small downstairs studio that they could rent out to a tenant. Since the space's lower floor was dark, a new opening was cut in the floor plate to allow light into a meeting room. This area, which also has a kitchen area and which allows access to the toilets, becomes the heart of the studio. Despite the fact that it has no windows, the use of colour swatches on the wall and in the custom-designed kitchen units brightens this potentially dark space, continuing what Nettleton describes as "our ongoing affair with colour".

Although the project had a tiny budget, Dive was able to create a very coherent aesthetic. For example, the Kartell lampshades above the meeting table are echoed by the use of large, bare lightbulbs elsewhere in the same proportions. The metal formwork of the concrete has been left exposed on the soffit and simply painted. Jacobsen furniture and Bulo chairs upstairs are contrasted with the galvanized handrails of the concrete stair and balustrade. In all, this interior is a sign of a young practice beginning to get its aesthetic concerns into focus, while providing eminently practical space.

EMI headquarters, Kensington, W8
MoreySmith

This major headquarters provides a cool and contemporary, but neutral, interior, which shows that you don't have to internalize radical thinking about office interiors to create a thoroughly pleasant place to work. This building, on Wright's Lane in Kensington, was formerly the headquarters of Penguin Books, and was taken over by EMI to unify their operations. The building now accommodates EMI Group headquarters, EMI Recorded Music global headquarters, EMI Recorded Music Continental Europe and EMI Classics, all of which previously occupied four separate buildings.

MoreySmith have comprehensively reworked the 1970s office building. The old façade is replaced by a curved glass frontage, through which the visitor enters into a new double-height reception area. A white render curved staircase leads up to the first floor, where a full-height atrium allows visual links across the entire layout. So often atriums can be soulless, dead places, but this one manages to buck the trend. The lifts have been left with their workings exposed, and a series of balconies and viewing points add animation. In addition, the floor of the atrium is used as a venue for musical events.

Each floor of offices is given its own identity through varying colour and material palettes, which extend also to the furniture used on each level. Break-out and refreshment areas are given some personality by eccentric juxtapositions of furniture – Chesterfield sofas go cheek by jowl with Eames loungers and Achille Castiglioni lighting.

The canteen features a glass counter illuminated by colour-changing LEDs, recalling the reception desk at the entrance. Opposite the counter a large graphic screen creates a sense of visual focus and complements the white tables and purple, grey and red chairs located in the main dining area. The space behind the counter is conceived as a 'snug' area, with walnut walls, bespoke leather sofas and pendant lighting.

Feilden Clegg Bradley office, Great Titchfield Street, W1
Plasma Studio

Young architects depend on the kudos from awards and competitions to start their practices, but it is not often the case that such accolades lead directly to a commission. However, this is exactly what happened to Plasma Studio after they won the Young Architect of the Year award in 2002.

This prestigious award was given to the practice on the back of little built work, but a wealth of theoretical projects that evinced their continuous-surface, folded aesthetic. In the lineage of Foreign Office Architects and UN Studio, Plasma are one of the most exciting of the current crop of designers using computer-generated complex forms. Richard Feilden, partner of architecture practice Feilden Clegg Bradley, was on the jury of the award, and decided to put his money where his mouth was by giving Plasma the job of refurbishing FCB's London offices in the West End.

The layout of the office is a U shape, with a new internal staircase connecting two corridors. The main interventions are large-scale pieces of furniture. The first is a new reception desk, which twists and turns to become a bench seat for visitors. (Workstations are at the same level as the reception desk, unifying the workspace and visitors' area.) The second is the new shelving system, one of the most visible parts of the project, which obscures views out of the building but displays models of the practice's works against the backdrop of the street. The perspex supports coincide with structural elements of the existing building and allow dappled daylight into the space. Perspex is also used for the new staircase, and is combined with plywood slabs to work as an extension of the display system.

Although alterations have been required since completion, they are in the spirit of the original design – proof of the strength of its aesthetic.

Fleishman Hillard office, Covent Garden, WC2
Walker & Martin

Walker & Martin is an architectural practice that describes itself as laid back, but that has worked at a range of scales, from door handles (for Allgood Ironmongery, featuring dimpled rubber pads) to offices for major advertising agency BBDO. It also considers itself an expert in call-centre design, and has undertaken a much-praised interior for holiday company Thomas Cook in Peterborough, which bucks the conventions of banks of seats filled with under-motivated staff. This experience was enough for Fleishman Hillard, the world's largest public relations agency, which was founded in America and now has a global reach.

Fleishman's London premises, while well located above Covent Garden tube station, presented a particular challenge: access was limited to a small ground-floor door beside a station used by thousands of visitors every day. The contractor described it as "like trying to do a loft conversion with site access through the letter box only".

Walker & Martin created a series of identifiably retro fit elements. One of the most striking of these is the huge, egg-shaped reception desk, behind which sits a circular, white, etched glass meeting room. These two sculptural pieces set the tone for the rest of the building and approach the holy grail of creative businesses – an environment that is business-like but encourages creative thought and the kind of people required for this type of work, who expect their lifestyles to be reflected in their workplaces.

The second, third and fourth floors provide predominantly open-plan office space, with some cellular offices and several glazed meeting rooms. The architects have managed to avoid suspended ceilings by providing workstations with integrated uplighters, which gives a degree of privacy and individuality and helps to differentiate the office environment. Air-conditioning and servicing pipes and ducts are left exposed. Pretty conventional finishes – plaster and carpet – round off the work space, but in the café, greater interest is provided by the floor-to-ceiling vinyl tile finishes.

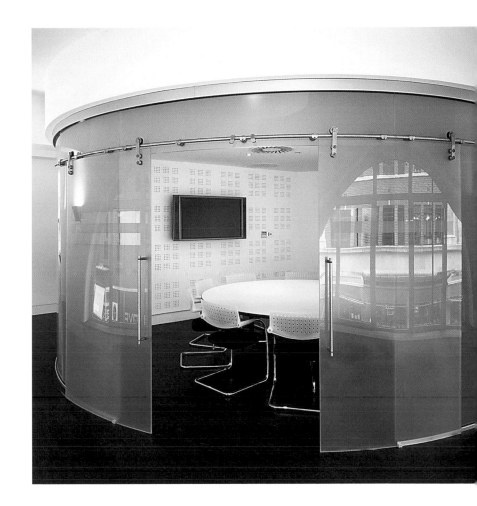

Institute of Directors, Pall Mall, SW1
Hemingway Design

The marriage of Wayne and Geraldine Hemingway with the Institute of Directors would seem an unlikely pairing at best. The Hemingways, co-founders of kitsch fashion house Red or Dead, had carried out few interior design projects since setting up Hemingway Design, and a dusty businessman's club in Pall Mall seemed an unusual place to start.

Wayne Hemingway has carved a certain antagonistic niche for himself in the architecture world, openly criticizing architects for their arrogance and taking a position in charge of styling mass housing for Wimpey Homes – another unlikely job. The story of Hemingway's initial contact with the institute has attained a mythic quality. The institute initially refused him entry because of his lack of a suit. He then returned, with TV cameras, dressed in accordance with the dress code – in a lady's pinstripe business suit.

The new lounge, branded as 'IoD at 123', is intended as a working area for those of the institute's 54,000 members who visit their London headquarters. It is very different in style from the more conventional surroundings at the institute's 116 Pall Mall premises, but hardly a cross-dressing transformation. The design emphasizes up-to-date working facilities and incorporates a number of measures that maximize the limited space. These include a cloakroom that can be stored in the wall and rolled out when needed and a large-scale mural that doubles as a flexible partition.

Hemingway's design reinterprets classic materials associated with the business world, such as pinstripe fabrics, polka dot carpets and bespoke furniture. Although much of it has the feel of an upmarket airport lounge, there are great touches that really break with convention, such as the timber-lined café area with its eccentric and gently humorous mural. The Red or Dead team haven't quite hit the heights of their fashion work with their interior design, but starting here – a business institute premises opened in 2001 by Tony Blair – should ensure that they have plenty more opportunities.

The Marketing Store, Covent Garden, WC2
Spence Harris Hogan Associates

Grappling with the tortuous world of advertising and marketing has been a difficult job for architecture and design. How can a building or interior, by definition something that has to last for some years, react to an industry that trades in trends lasting a matter of weeks? There are many examples of buildings that express brand identities, but as brands have to be ever nimbler and faster moving, how can architecture keep up?

One of the solutions often employed by contemporary architects and designers is to give a company a changing shop window that reflects the values of the company without having to come up with a static logo or identity. This is exactly what SHH have done for The Marketing Store, a company that claims to work in the dark arts of "brand activation".

The low-budget transformation of an unprepossessing shopfront in Covent Garden attempts to make the reception area into part of the public realm. The office is very close to Covent Garden tube station, which was recognized as a place where people meet up before going out to the bars and restaurants in the area. Capitalizing on this, SHH made a shop window for the company with three semi-transparent timber-framed screens inserted into the existing glass façade, allowing different degrees of privacy. When open, the screens reveal a light installation made up of cold cathode lights with a rolling pattern of illumination in the corporate colours of the client, avoiding static representations of the Marketing Store brand and intended to attract the eye of passers-by.

This playful installation allows the more modest materials of the rest of the lobby – timber and glass – to recede from view. However, there are more witty touches, such as the television stand in the form of a carrier bag – the logo of the company.

This is not the most sophisticated response to the high-technology future of branding and marketing, but it does show that, at all ends of the market, the way in which a brand occupies a building is changing to something more fluid, having more in common with the 'viral marketing' of the internet age than the traditional advertising media of billboards and shop signs.

Lobby for McGraw Hill, Canary Wharf, E14
Danny Lane/SOM

The offices of Canary Wharf are an object lesson in new corporate architecture, ranging from the Postmodernism of Cesar Pelli's Canary Wharf tower to the high-tech of Norman Foster's buildings for Citibank and HSBC. What they all have in common are atriums, the bigger the better – a lesson learnt from the corporate architecture of New York and Chicago in providing the illusion of public space in the privately owned business ghetto.

Artist and designer Danny Lane rose to prominence in the 1980s when he pioneered the use of structural glass in furniture. He has been quiet since, privately developing the technical knowledge that enables him to produce works on the scale of this one – a 22-tonne installation in the lobby of SOM's 20 Canada Square building, to be occupied by the publishing group McGraw Hill. This northerly entrance is spatially not the most impressive at Canary Wharf, but Lane's sculpture makes it one of the most interesting.

This was the first in a series of pieces that form something of a comeback tour for Lane. Other recent commissions include works in Newcastle and Gateshead, and a four-piece iron and glass work at the Paddington Basin office development in west London.

The piece for McGraw Hill, entitled *The Parting of the Waves*, is an undulating ribbon of glass 4 m high and 10 m long (13 x 32 ft) running the length of each side of the entrance. Costing £200,000, the installation is made up of 2000 narrow strips of glass, which are not bonded, but held in place by gravity and by clips at the top and bottom. The industrial-grade glass transmits light through its edges, forming an intriguing mix of transparent and light-emitting properties. The only criticism to be made of the piece is that the lobby beyond this link to the street seems rather bland in comparison.

Squire and Partners office, Wicklow Street, WC1
Squire and Partners

At a time when architects earn very little compared to most other professions, their primary means of making serious money can often come from seeing the potential in a property, occupying it and refurbishing it themselves. Squire and Partners, an eighty-strong practice originally based in Kensington, has done exactly this, turning an unprepossessing former car park in King's Cross into a very contemporary office space.

Squire and Partners is a proficient architectural practice that has been peddling its brand of cool and corporate modernism for over twenty five years. With their own office, they have applied the hard-nosed pragmatism of commercial development, along with touches of levity and the virtuosity that comes with experience.

The site was a basement and ground floor of a 1930s factory on Wicklow Street, near King's Cross station. The floors above had already been converted into housing, but the bottom two floors had low ceilings that made them unattractive for any use other than car parking. They also contained the service pipes of the housing above, all of which had to be relocated before work could begin in earnest.

The design responded to the ceiling height issue by removing the ground floor and casting a new, thinner concrete slab that is set back from the front elevation, creating a double-height space at the front and allowing natural light into the basement floor. The new ground-floor-level mezzanine is connected to the street by a rather camp glass bridge. More attractive are the beautiful precast concrete staircases with their offset spines, engineered by Price & Myers, that lead from the reception areas to the lower ground studio. The more pragmatic aspects of the project are also beautifully done, with storage behind etched glass doors and simple white desks mixed with classic, if very familiar, Modernist chairs.

Not only has this interior made a generous space to work, but it has also given a presence on the street, with huge bespoke glass panes forming a kind of shopfront, through which passers-by can peer. Squire and Partners has continued in its role as developer–architect with 6 St Chad's Place (see pages 50–51), a bar just yards from their headquarters. Although there is nothing astonishing about this office project, it shows how the intelligent use of a leftover basement can create fantastic working conditions.

Nike office
Jump Studios

Jump Studios has all the requisite qualifications to design the headquarters for one of the world's biggest brands: a multi-disciplinary background, a cool Hoxton address, an office in Italy and a track record in its short history of making extremely trendy interiors to demonstrate the values of brands in an understated or innovative way. Their stand for Levi's at the 2003 Pitti Uomo fashion fair in Italy, for example, chose to take the company away from its traditional image and incorporated an antique loom in the centre of the stall, along with rolls of red fabric.

Jump's directors boast a range of talents – two are architects, two had worked previously for Ron Arad designing furniture, and one had worked in advertising as a brand consultant. Their headquarters for Nike, in an undisclosed location, integrate this diverse expertise with subtlety and showmanship.

The building contains offices and engineering studios for Nike, but also showrooms for buyers to look at the products. Much of the project, therefore, concerns the display of various Nike ranges. This is done in a series of racks on the wall and in wire cages, which also give the space a more intimate, retail-like atmosphere than an ordinary office. The branding is pretty subtle, with perhaps just the geometry of the curves of the walls referring to the iconic Nike swoosh.

The colour scheme is broadly blue, including the waiting room, with its resin floors and custom-designed furniture, and visuals on the wall of Nike-sponsored sports stars such as Ronaldo or Tiger Woods. Spatially the scheme is intended to give a sense of intimacy, while allowing the more secret parts of the operation to remain private. The curved conference room is always visible from every part of the floorplate, giving visual focus and a sense of excitement to the regular rows of workstations.

Seymour Powell office, Fulham, SW6
Barr Gazetas

When designers become clients, the outcome is not always a happy one. Despite demanding control over design with their own clients, there is often an unwillingness to cede it when they employ external consultants.

Architects Barr Gazetas could barely have ended up with a higher-profile designer client than Seymour Powell. This consultancy was started by Richard Seymour and Dick Powell, who have since risen to prominence as two of the TV-friendly faces of design. The products they have designed during their twenty-year association range from bras to motorcycles.

Seymour Powell had outgrown its previous offices, and Barr Gazetas was given the task of refurbishing a disused joinery workshop, unifying prototyping workshop and design offices in the process. The project extended the existing building to form a complex arranged around a courtyard.

The interior is arranged around the office of the two partners, who face each other across a huge shared desk in a top-floor eyrie. The transparency of the materials used internally – glass and minimal steel balustrading – means that the potential hierarchical implications (the bosses presiding over the factory floor) are diminished, and the simple, open-tread staircase adds to this feeling.

Another key feature of the interior is a space on the ground floor where prototypes from previous Seymour Powell projects are displayed in a gallery-like setting. Pristine white rendered walls hold the objects set in glass cases (conceived as 'jewellery boxes'), creating a strong contrast with the bare brick interior walls of the existing industrial building and recalling the white of its exterior.

The main studio floor is in the roof, but the low ceilings and potentially cramped dimensions are liberated by huge skylights, which provide the indirect light ideal for a design studio. These are finished with a series of bookcases designed by Barr Gazetas in collaboration with Seymour Powell.

The result is a calm and collected interior, with a satisfying contrast between intimate, individual spaces and the larger areas of the studios.

Valtech office, Clerkenwell, EC1
Harper Mackay

The dotcom explosion in the mid–late 1990s saw a proliferation of office spaces that bucked the overriding trend of standard suspended ceilings, carpet tiles and dull workstations. These new and wealthy companies demanded a working atmosphere that would help them retain staff in a volatile marketplace, and provide identity at a time when companies' life spans were not as long as they might be.

Valtech, a large e-business, commissioned Harper Mackay to design its London headquarters with a brief to create an environment that reflected their business, and that would make an immediate impact on visitors. They also wanted a building that would allow employees to feel part of a community.

The architect conceived an interior that could constantly change, but that theatrically expressed the desires of the employees with a series of outsize graphics on the walls. The café area, for example, was thought of as a clearing in a forest, with large-scale photographs of a romantic copse on the walls. This is an oblique reference to the company's Stockholm office, which is surrounded by trees, and is very popular with employees.

The most publicized part of the project is probably the toilets, which continue the themes of the rest of the office and are decorated with vistas of the Swiss Alps, the Golden Gate Bridge and New York City. All of these graphics are in inexpensive but durable materials, and can be changed by Valtech as often as required.

The architect's first idea was to create an ultimately flexible environment out of a series of curtains. This was rejected, but something of this feeling has been retained in the corrugated polycarbonate panelling used in the training area and the honeycomb panelling elsewhere. The Lensvelt storage system is also used as partitioning in places. Social space is key at Valtech, and there is a high proportion of areas for repose rather than work, including a self-service breakfast bar with a Philippe Starck dining table, and a computer games area.

Victoria House, Holborn, WC1
Alsop Architects

Victoria House has been a building awaiting conversion by Alsop Architects for some years. The huge office building – which occupies an entire block and forms one side of Bloomsbury Square – was built in the 1930s for an insurance company, and was at one point a candidate to accommodate the Greater London Assembly, before it occupied Norman Foster's glassy egg near Tower Bridge.

Alsop's project as built is a speculative office development and exists as a watered-down version of the open spaces and bombastic hanging pods that feature in his design for the GLA. This is largely because the requirements of large amounts of floor space for the offices have meant that the pods are rather more like withered internal organs than the pulsing heart of the building.

However, the new layout, arranged around two atriums (which accommodate the pods), makes for a very nice workplace indeed. The white rendered blobs reflect light into the deepest recesses of the floorplates, and the high atriums perform environmentally, creating a naturally ventilated common area, saving energy despite the individual floors being air-conditioned.

Some original internal features of the building have been retained and refurbished, including the stairwells, the beautiful Art Deco ballroom (which will be a restaurant) and a series of wood-panelled offices, which are marketed as "heritage suites". There are places where the junction between old and new is less comfortable – the beautiful glazed bricks of the atriums have been covered with glass louvres, and the floating glass floor in the main reception area provides disabled access but obscures the original inlaid floor.

Will Alsop is one of the highest-profile names in British architecture and is capable of more excitement than this. His colourful Peckham library is proof of that. It seems that the business world has not accepted Alsop's blobs so much as made them conform to a corporate dress code.

Further reading

The Architecture Foundation, *New Architects 2: A Guide to Britain's Best Young Architectural Practices*, London (Merrell) 2001

Juanita Cheung, *Drink London: Architecture and Alcohol*, London (BT Batsford) 2000

Caroline Constant, *Eileen Gray*, London and New York (Phaidon) 2002

Luca Deon and Tony Hafliger, *Caruso St John Architects: Knitting Weaving Wrapping Pressing*, Basel (Birkhäuser) 2002

Marcus Field and Mark Irving, *Lofts*, London (Laurence King) 2001

Mark Girouard, *Victorian Pubs*, Cambridge MA (Yale University Press) 1984

David Heathcote, *Penthouse Over the City: The Barbican and Modern Living*, Chichester (Wiley-Academy) 2004

Edwin Heathcote, *London Caffs*, Chichester (Wiley-Academy) 2004

Joe Kerr and Andrew Gibson (eds.), *London from Punk to Blair*, London (Reaktion) 2003

Martin Kunz, *London*, Kempen (teNeues) 2004

Kieran Long, Kester Rattenbury and Robert Bevan, *Architects Today*, London (Laurence King) 2004

John Pawson, *John Pawson: Themes and Projects*, London and New York (Phaidon) 2002

Kenneth Powell, *New London Architecture*, London (Merrell) 2003

Andreas Ruby, Angeli Sachs and Philip Ursprung, *Minimal Architecture*, Munich (Prestel) 2003

Courtenay Smith and Annette Ferrara, *Xtreme Interiors*, Munich (Prestel) 2003

Thomas Weaver (ed.), *David Chipperfield Architectural Works 1990–2002*, New York (Princeton Architectural Press) 2003

John Welsh, *Modern House*, London and New York (Phaidon) 1999

Richard Weston, *The House in the 20th Century*, London (Laurence King) 2002

Picture credits

Acknowledgements

The illustrations in this book have been reproduced courtesy of the following copyright holders:

Alsop Architects pp. 232–33; Arcaid pp. 134–35; Arcblue pp. 20–21; Sue Barr pp. 154–55, 172–73, 192, 198–99; BDP/Niall Clutton pp. 13–14; Hélène Binet pp. 2, 113, 118–21, 128–29, 160–65, 168–69; Charles Birchmore pp. 62–63; Block Architecture pp. 38–39; Tim Brotherton pp. 36–37, 44–45, 102, 106–07; Richard Bryant/Arcaid pp. 194–95; Joseph Burns pp. 48–49, 76–77; Burrell Foley Fischer pp. 116–17; Caulder Moore pp. 79, 104–05; Leon Chew p. 46; Philip Christou p. 157 (top); David Churchill pp. 208–09; Cloud 9 Photography for McDonald's Restaurants Ltd p. 12; Peter Cook/View pp. 182–83; Corbis p. 19 (right); Alan Crow/View pp. 184–85; Rolant Dafis pp. 24, 30–31, 47, 52–53; Richard Davies pp. 26–27, 66, 87, 96–97, 178 (middle), 179; Andy Day pp. 80–81; Gaultier DeBlonde p. 112; Guy Drayton p. 130; El Ultimo Grito pp. 82–83; Eurostar Corporate Communications pp. 34–35; Foster and Partners pp. 17–18; Future Systems pp. 88–89; Chris Gascoigne pp. 206–07; David Grandorge pp. 70, 90–91, 156, 157 (middle), 157 (bottom), 188–89; Peter Gunzel pp. 214–15; Harper Mackay pp. 84–85, 202–03, 230–31; Hufton & Crow p. 73; Richard Hywel Evans pp. 186–87; Institute of Directors pp. 218–19; Alun Jones pp. 166–67; Jump pp. 226–27; Nicholas Kane pp. 50–51, 114, 132–33, 136–37, 174–77; Christopher Kicherer pp. 74–75; Gunnar Knetchel pp. 58–59; Jose Lasheras pp. 152, 190–91; www.leonardo.com p. 124; Manser Practice pp. 54–55; John McAslan + Partners pp. 94–95; Louise Melchior pp. 92–93; Louise Melchior/Lara Gosling pp. 100–01; Minus One pp. 180–81; Philippe Moseley jacket front, pp. 158–59; OMA pp. 15–16; Eric Parry pp. 136–37, 174–75; John Pawson pp. 8–9; Powell Tuck pp. 200–01; Ed Reeve pp. 68–69; David Ripley p. 141; Saatchi Gallery p. 10; Robert Sakula pp. 126–27; Shed 54 p. 140; Jefferson Smith pp. 210–11; Timothy Soar pp. 150–51; Soho House Ltd p. 125; Dan Stevens p. 86; Edmund Sumner/VIEW p. 131; Super Potato pp. 64–65; Tank Design pp. 98–99; Peter Tarry pp. 196–97; Thorp Design pp. 108–09; Paul Tyagi pp. 146–47, 178 (top), 178 (bottom), 204–05; VIEW pp. 19 (left), 32–33, 71, 72, 110–11, 212–13, 224–25; Victoria and Albert Museum p. 22; Morley von Sternberg pp. 42–43; Walker & Martin pp. 216–17; Matthew Weinreb/www.imagefind.com pp. 138–39; Wells Mackereth pp. 28–29, 56–57, 60–61; Wingate & Moon p. 78; Peter Wood pp. 222–23; Carley Wright pp. 148–49; Francesca Yorke pp. 122–23, 170–71, 220–21, 228–29; Nigel Young pp. 142, 144–45; Herbert Ypma pp. 40–41

The publisher has made every effort to trace and contact copyright holders of the illustrations reproduced in this book; they will be happy to correct in subsequent editions any errors or omissions that are brought to their attention.

I would like to thank Julian Honer and Hugh Merrell at Merrell Publishers for their initial faith and support, and Sam Wythe for managing an excellent editing process. Caroline Thomas managed the picture research extremely successfully, and thanks are due to the architects and designers for providing information and pictures.

Thanks, for continuing support and inspiration, to Michael Howe, Patrick Lynch and Claudia Murin, Daniel Rosbottom and Schirin Taraz. I am grateful to Marcus Fairs, Chris Hall and all at Icon magazine who allowed me the time to complete the text despite the pressures of a monthly publication. Thanks also to Building Design magazine for early help from its library and to the staff of the RIBA library. Special thanks are due to my father, Colin Long, and my sister, Joanne Long, who provided heroic help with the final leg of collecting information.

This book is dedicated to William de Peyer and Alex Liakos, who have made London make sense to me, inside and out.

Kieran Long
London 2004

Index

First published 2004 by Merrell Publishers Limited

Head office
42 Southwark Street
London SE1 1UN

New York office
49 West 24th Street, 8th floor
New York, NY 10010

www.merrellpublishers.com

Publisher Hugh Merrell
Editorial Director Julian Honer
US Director Joan Brookbank
Sales and Marketing Director Emilie Amos
Sales and Marketing Executive Emily Sanders
Managing Editor Anthea Snow
Editor Sam Wythe
Design Manager Nicola Bailey
Production Manager Michelle Draycott
Design and Production Assistant Matt Packer

British Library Cataloguing-in-Publication Data:
Long, Kieran
New London interiors
1. Interior decoration – England – London
2. Interior architecture – England – London
I. Title
747'.09421

ISBN 1 85894 237 3

Produced by Merrell Publishers
Designed by Keith Lovegrove
Copy-edited by Caroline Ball
Indexed by Christine Shuttleworth
Printed and bound in Slovenia by Mladinska knjiga-tiskarna

Jacket front: Beck penthouse, Docklands, E14 (see pages 158–59)
Jacket back, left to right: Grand Central bar, Great Eastern Street, EC2
(see pages 38–39); Bartle Bogle Hegarty office, Soho, W1 (see pages
198–99)

Page 2: House, Blythe Road, Hammersmith (see pages 168–69)
Page 6: Apartment, Hampstead, NW3 (see pages 156–57)
Page 24: Silka restaurant, Borough Market, SE1 (see pages 52–53)
Page 66: Marni boutique, Sloane Street, SW3 (see page 87)
Page 102: Fordham White hair salon, Soho, W1 (see pages 106–07)
Page 114: The Saatchi Gallery, County Hall, SE1 (see pages 132–33)
Page 142: London School of Economics library, Aldwych, WC2 (see
pages 144–45)
Page 152: Lasheras studio, Shoreditch, N1 (see pages 190–91)
Page 192: Bartle Bogle Hegarty office, Soho, W1 (see pages 198–99)